To —
Jennifer
Best Wishes and Blue Skies Always!))

THE BIRDS
WERE
SILVER THEN

STORIES OF THE VIETNAM AIR WAR
EDITED AND TOLD BY
LOWELL PETERSON

Lowell Peterson

2009

First Edition

ISBN Number: 0-9719128-3-1

Library of Congress Number: 2006935353

Published by:

PETERSON HOUSE
2627 Beechwood Court
Appleton, WI 54911
SRoseClear@aol.com

Book cover and design by

GRAPHIC LIAISONS, LLC
Waupaca, WI 54981
www.graphicliaisons.com

Printed in the United States by
WORZALLA PUBLISHING COMPANY
Stevens Point, WI 54481
www.worzalla.com

This book is dedicated to the
American warriors who fought in the air war
over North Vietnam.
They join the long line of patriots
who have defended democracy
and freedom throughout the history
of the American nation.
May God perpetuate their belief in
"Duty, Honor, Country"
for generations to come.

CONTENTS

I

PEACETIME INNOCENCE—FIRST ENCOUNTERS, 1960 - 1964

by Lowell Peterson

II

COMBAT DEPLOYMENT—AUGUST 1964 - JUNE 1965 IN THEIR OWN WORDS

(Stories related with their rank at the time of the events.)

III
THE TURNING POINT, JULY 24 - 27, 1965

IV
CAPTIVITY AND TORTURE

V
REQUIEM TO WAR

VI
VIGNETTES OF AIR FORCE LIFE, 1963 - 1966

BIOGRAPHIES

COLOR SECTION

ACKNOWLEDGMENTS

I believe the time is right and the public is ready to re-examine the Vietnam era. It is my hope that you who lived it, those of you who can't remember it because you were too young, and those of you who were not yet born will critically examine the chronicles of one of the most difficult periods in the annals of United States history. I want you to immerse yourself in the subject and try to feel the emotions I felt then and still feel today.

First and foremost, I wish to thank the pilots of the 18th Tactical Fighter Wing, the 12th Tactical Fighter Squadron, the 44th Tactical Fighter Squadron, the 67th Tactical Fighter Squadron, the 15th Tactical Reconnaissance Squadron, and the squadrons from McConnell Air Force Base, for their pivotal role in the air war over North Vietnam. Their willingness to share their experiences was a generous gift to me and to future generations. I'm forever grateful to them.

Secondly, I wish to acknowledge the invaluable contribution of Kitty O'Callaghan, a freelance writer in White Plains, New York, who edited the manuscript. Her insistence on clarity and consistency were priceless in moving this project forward. Likewise, Jim Peterson deserves my gratitude for his willingness to read the entire first draft, and for taking more time from his corporate law practice than he could spare to make insightful suggestions. Both Kitty and Jim helped me shape the disparate voices of the different chapters into a cohesive story, and I am proud of the result we achieved. I am also proud to acknowledge that they are my children.

I'd be remiss if I didn't recognize the efforts of Vi Stoner whose copy-editing talent polished my words and covered my tracks, preventing the reader from discovering my fondness for long compound sentences and misplaced commas. Also making me look good were Camin Potts and Marcia Lorenzen of Graphic Liaisons, LLC, who readied the book for publication. No less important were the contributions of my other children, Erik Peterson and Dr. Linda Peterson, whose insightful questions and positive support led to various improvements in the text. Finally, I would like to acknowledge the valuable assistance of my wife, Mary, for her critical review of the manuscript, and for her undying patience while I spent long hours writing and editing.

Lowell Peterson

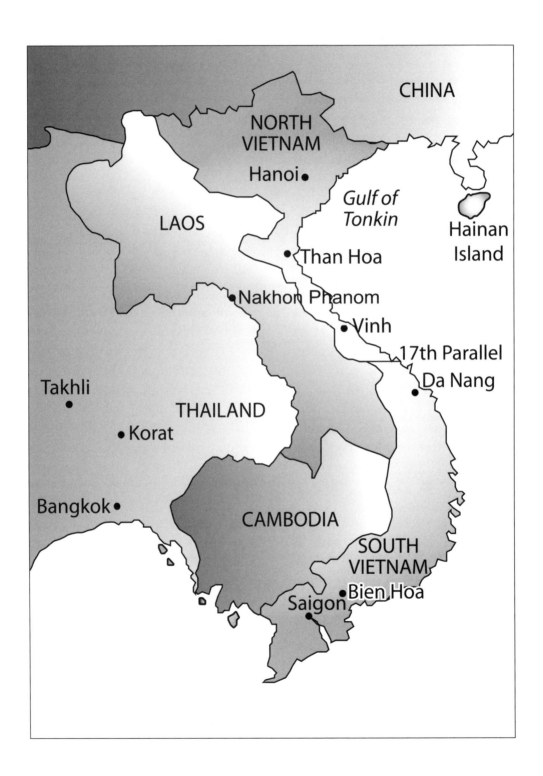

TIMELINE

September 2, 1945—World War II in the Pacific officially ends.

September 2, 1945—Ho Chi Minh declares independence of Vietnam.

1946-1954—Indochina War between France and Vietnam.

October 1949—Chinese Communists defeat Nationalist China.

1950—Korean War begins.

1950—The Soviet Union officially recognizes the Communist North Vietnamese Vietminh Party.

1954—Geneva Peace Accord divides North and South Vietnam at the 17th Parallel.

May 7, 1954—France surrenders at Dien Bien Phu.

December 1960—National Liberation Front (NLF) organized—(Viet Cong).

January 1961—John F. Kennedy takes office as President of the United States.

Spring 1961—President John F. Kennedy authorizes 100 advisors and 400 Special Forces Troops to train the South Vietnamese Army in counterinsurgency.

December 1961—3,205 U.S. advisors are in South Vietnam.

October 1962—The Cuban missile crisis occurs.

December 1962—9,000 U.S. advisors are in South Vietnam.

November 1, 1963—South Vietnam's government overthrown and Premier Ngo Dinh Diem is murdered.

November 22, 1963—John F. Kennedy assassinated; Lyndon B. Johnson becomes President of the United States.

January 29, 1964—General Nguyen Khan overthrows General Duong Van Minh and becomes Premier of South Vietnam.

August 1, 1964—Gulf of Tonkin incident occurs.

August 4, 1964—Second Tonkin incident reportedly occurs.

August 5, 1964—First U.S. air attack flown against North Vietnam.

December 1964—23,300 U.S. advisors are in South Vietnam; $50 million in aid delivered to South Vietnam this year.

February 7, 1965—Viet Cong attack Pleiku killing nine U.S. soldiers and destroying five airplanes; President Johnson orders operation Flaming Dart to attack military installations north of the 17th Parallel.

February 10, 1965—Viet Cong attack American enlisted men's barracks at Qui Nhon.

February 11, 1965—President Johnson orders operation Rolling Thunder, a sustained air attack reprisal on North Vietnam.

March 8, 1965—Two battalions of United States Marines land at Da Nang to protect the U.S. air base.

April 1965—3,600 sorties are flown against North Vietnam by U.S. aircraft.

May 1965—4,000 sorties are flown against North Vietnam by U.S. aircraft.

July 1965—President Johnson commits the U.S. to war and sends 50,000 ground troops to Vietnam.

1965—25,000 sorties are flown against North Vietnam by U.S. aircraft.

1965—A total of 190,000 U.S. troops are in South Vietnam by the end of the year.

July 24, 1965—First surface-to-air missile (SAM) attack on U.S. airplanes flying over North Vietnam occurs.

July 27, 1965—President Johnson orders operation Iron Hand, a mass reprisal U.S. air attack against SAM missile sites in North Vietnam.

1966—U.S. troops in South Vietnam increase to 300,000 and 79,000 air sorties are flown by the end of the year.

1967—108,000 U.S. air sorties flown in this year.

January 21, 1968—Khe Sanh comes under attack by Viet Cong and Viet Minh.

January 31, 1968—Viet Cong and Viet Minh launch the TET offensive.

March 30, 1968—Lyndon B. Johnson announces to the nation that he will not accept the nomination for another term as President of the United States.

March 31, 1968—A U.S. bombing halt is ordered below the 20th Parallel.

April 1, 1968—United States Secretary of Defense Robert S. McNamara resigns.

November 1, 1968—Peace Talks begin in Paris.

January 1969—Richard M. Nixon takes office as President of the United States.

1970—U.S. troop strength reduced to 280,000 in South Vietnam.

November 21, 1970—U.S. raid on Son Tay prison in North Vietnam.

1971—U.S. troop strength reduced to 140,000 in South Vietnam.

1972—U.S. troop strength reduced to 70,000 in South Vietnam.

November 1972—Richard M. Nixon elected to second term as President of United States.

December 18, 1972—Operation Linebacker II begins—intense U.S. B-52 attacks on Hanoi and surrounding areas.

February 11, 1973—U.S. POWs released from North Vietnam.

June 1973—U.S. troop strength reduced to 250 Americans; U.S. aid to South Vietnam $1.4 billion in 1973.

August 9, 1974—Nixon resigns presidency; Gerald Ford becomes President of the United States.

1974—Congress reduces U.S. aid to South Vietnam to $700 million; North Vietnam deploys 350,000 troops into South Vietnam in violation of the Paris Agreements.

April 21, 1975—Nguyen Van Thieu resigns as Premier when the U.S. Congress refuses to provide further aid to South Vietnam; he flies to Taipei, Taiwan, with 3 1/2 tons of gold.

April 30, 1975—President Gerald Ford orders U.S. ambassador Graham Martin out of South Vietnam.

May 1, 1975—Saigon falls to the Viet Cong and Viet Minh.

FOREWORD

*People are human; they are fallible. I concede with painful
candor and a heavy heart that the adage applies to me and to my
generation of American leadership regarding Vietnam. Although
we sought to do the right thing—and believed we were doing the
right thing—in my judgement, hindsight proves us wrong.*

Robert S. McNamara
1995

The stories you are about to read are very personal. They reflect on the era of the Vietnam War, often berated as one of the most tragic and depressing epochs in the history of the United States. The stories also reflect on the experiences of the fighter pilots who lived the story day-in and day-out for almost ten years in the air war over North Vietnam. The stories in this book are representative of what it was like in those early years of the war when the "birds" (F-105s) were still silver.

I have cared for critically ill patients as a medical doctor and cardiologist for more than thirty-five years and in this profession have known the exhilaration of success as well as the tragedy of failure. But, as a Flight Surgeon in the United States Air Force from 1963 to 1966, I also experienced professional satisfaction, personal happiness, and intense pride in my mission. God graciously put me in a place to play a role in an era in history that will be reviewed, discussed, disputed, and massaged by historians for generations to come.

In every walk of life, it is usually the people you have the honor of being associated with, what they mean to you, and what you mean to them that creates satisfaction. I had the privilege to be associated with the United States Air Force F-105 fighter pilots, who were asked to put their lives on the line, unselfishly, frighteningly, and professionally, in a war they knew they could, but were not allowed, to win. They would face death, imprisonment, torture, abuse from their fellow citizens, objective dishonor, and eventually defeat at the hands of an inferior, nationalistic-motivated fighting force. We, the United States Air Force, Pacific Air Force (PACAF), 5th Air Force, the 313th Air Division, the 18th TAC Fighter Wing, the 12th, 44th, and 67th TAC Fighter Squadrons, the 15th TAC Recon Squadron had our war, and we were committed to do our job to the best of our ability. We accepted the challenge, and in spite of adversity, came home proud of what we had done, but sick in-the-pit of our stomachs at what we could not do. The United States Air Force personnel I served with can look the American public straight in the eye and say, "We deserve your honor."

Yes, the Vietnam War, and especially the air war over North Vietnam, was very personal. It was then; it is now. I hope, as you read these stories, you will understand what these dedicated men did for you and for your country at one of the lowest points in its entire history. I hope I can convey the message in this book in such a way that the Vietnam War, and particularly the air war over North Vietnam becomes very personal for you as well.

PREFACE

For every one of yours we kill, you will kill ten of ours,
but in the end it is you who will grow tired.
                    Ho Chi Minh
                    1946

It is nigh impossible to believe the United States was not fully aware of the history of Vietnam and its greater than 2,000 years of strife and struggle in nation building. Perhaps the U.S. Government thought our involvement in Vietnam would be different than what the Vietnamese had experienced under the iron hand of the Chinese, under the Mongolian, Kublai Khan, under their ancient warlords, under the colonial rule of France, or under the military rule of Japan. It would prove not to be so.

A short modern-day history of this land through the latter half of the nineteenth century and the first two-thirds of the twentieth century serves as a backdrop for how the United States became engaged in the Vietnam War.

Nineteenth century colonial expansionism by European nations did not spare Vietnam and Indochina. In 1858, France invaded South Vietnam, gaining complete control in 1867. The French then went on to conquer North Vietnam in 1883 and to take control of Kampuchea (latter day Cambodia) and Laos.

With the defeat of France by Germany in 1940, all of Indochina was seized by Japan, a German ally, and it remained under Japanese control until the end of World War II. When the war was over in 1945, Ho Chi Minh, a Vietnamese communist revolutionary, supported by his allies—General Giap, the Vietminh party of fellow revolutionaries, and a coalition of non-Communist anti-French nationalists—gained control and proclaimed Vietnam independent. It was renamed the Democratic Republic of Vietnam (DRV).

The French, like other European nations, still had a colonial mindset after World War II and returned to Southeast Asia after the defeat of Germany and Japan. In December 1946, the Indochina War between France and the Vietminh began. During this war, the United States funded about forty percent of the French effort. The United States not only considered Indochina as an area of economic and strategic importance, but also reviled Ho Chi Minh as a communist directed by the Soviet Union—not just a nationalist freedom fighter. The threat of communist Russia to the security of Europe and the rest of the free world during the Cold War led American policymakers to support France in general, but particularly in Indochina.

When the Nationalist Chinese Government of Chiang Kai-shek was defeated by the Chinese communist army of Mao Tse-tung in 1949, the United States feared Chinese communist influence on Vietnam and all of Indochina. The Korean War began in 1950, with the Soviet Union supporting its North Korean ally. When the Chinese entered the war, the United States extrapolated this to a communist domination by a Russian-Chinese alliance that would spread throughout Asia, Southeast Asia, and the world—the so-called Domino Theory.

> *You have a row of dominoes set up, you knock over the first one*
> *and the last one will go over quickly.*
> Dwight D. Eisenhower
> 1954

By early 1954, extensive negotiations between the United States Congress, the State Department, and President Eisenhower were carried out to determine whether the United States should send troops to Vietnam. But, because trade and treaty concessions from France were not forthcoming, and Great Britain was not eager to involve itself in the conflict, the entire burden to lend support fell to the United States. A peace settlement, arranged by major world powers at the urging of the United States, was negotiated between France and the Vietminh at Geneva, but before this could be implemented, the Vietminh army under the command of General Giap defeated the French at Dien Bien Phu on May 7, 1954.

After the hostilities ceased between France and the Vietminh, the Geneva Peace Conference decided to divide Vietnam at the 17th Parallel into North Vietnam and South Vietnam. As a result of this agreement in 1955, Ngo Dinh Diem was elected leader of South Vietnam, establishing the Republic of Vietnam (RVN), while Ho Chi Minh remained in control of the North.

By 1956 the United States had assumed, from France, full responsibility for training the South Vietnamese Army through the Joint United States Military Assistance and Advisory Group (JUSMAAG) based in Saigon, the capital of the new South Vietnam. The JUSMAAG had six hundred ninety-two American military advisors.

In 1957, Vietminh insurgents from North Vietnam and sympathizers in South Vietnam rebelled against the Diem government and became organized as the National Liberation Front or Viet Cong. By 1960 the Viet Cong were openly encouraged by North Vietnam to begin an armed struggle against Diem. By late 1962, the Viet Cong had gained three hundred thousand members and a passive following of more than one million. As the RVN government fell deeper into disarray, Diem became more dictatorial and oppressive in his policies. Buddhists joined in opposition to Diem, supporting uprisings and attempted coups against the strongly Catholic RVN government, which included several Diem family members, particularly his brother, Ngo Dinh Nhu, and his wife, the "Dragon Lady", Madame Nhu.

In 1961, because of increasing aggression by North and South Vietnamese communists, President John F. Kennedy authorized one hundred more advisors and four hundred special forces troops be sent to South Vietnam. American military assistance more than doubled between 1961 and 1962, including shipments of armor and military aircraft.

> If we withdrew from Vietnam, the communists would control Vietnam;
> pretty soon, Thailand, Laos, Cambodia, Malaya, would go …
> John F. Kennedy
> 1962

By the end of 1962, more than nine-thousand advisors, an eight-fold increase, were in Vietnam. The Cuban Missile Crisis of October 1962 temporarily diverted the attention of the United States from the conflict in Southeast Asia, but the die was cast for an ever-expanding conflict that would go on for the next thirteen years.

> We held off the French for eight years; we can hold off the Americans
> for at least as long. Americans don't like long, inconclusive wars.
> This is going to be a long inconclusive war.
> Ho Chi Minh
> 1962

On November 1, 1963, a coup by army generals toppled the Diem government while the U.S. Government looked the other way. Both Diem and his brother Nhu were captured and murdered. The revolt was led by Duong Van Minh and a junta of twelve army officers who also proved to be ineffective in running the government. On January 29, 1964, another group of officers led by General Nguyen Khan, succeeded in dislodging Minh. One year later, Khan likewise was forced to resign, and after a series of interim governments, Vice Air Marshal Nguyen Cao Ky assumed control of South Vietnam. *Time* magazine reported on July 16, 1965, that

Henry Cabot Lodge had replaced Maxwell Taylor as United States ambassador to South Vietnam, who in turn had replaced Lodge a year earlier. When Lodge initially left on June 29, 1964, Major General Nguyen Khanh was premier. By the time he returned there had been six changes of government and the current Premier incumbent was Air Commodore Nguyen Cao Ky. Political instability in South Vietnam continued throughout the war, forcing both the United States and South Vietnam to pursue military solutions, rather than political ones.

> *In South Vietnam, the U.S. has stumbled into a bog.*
> *It will be mired there for a long time.*
> Nikita Kruschev
> U.S.S.R.
> 1962

By the time of the Gulf of Tonkin incident in August 1964, the U.S. advisors in Vietnam had risen to twenty-three thousand, three-hundred. The first Tonkin incident happened at 1230 hours, August 1, 1964, when the *USS Maddox* destroyer sailing in the Gulf of Tonkin was attacked by unidentified surface craft from the direction of Hon Me island. Guns and torpedoes were fired at the *Maddox*, which responded, destroying one boat with a missile. F-8 Crusader aircraft from the carrier *USS Ticonderoga*, destroyed the remaining boats as they retreated. At 2152 hours on August 4, gunboats were again reportedly sighted approaching from the direction of the Vietnam coast. In the oily-black, moonless night, in reality or in imagination, the sea battle commenced.

> *The infamous pretext for leaping headlong into the Vietnam War was the Gulf of Tonkin incident. My old destroyer, the USS Maddox, (WWII service) was patrolling the Gulf of Tonkin 25 miles off the coast of North Vietnam … when it was attacked … two days later the USS Maddox … reported that it was under attack again … when I read the dispatches five years later as Secretary of Defense, there was no second attack. There was confusion, hysteria, and miscommunication on a dark night … . McNamara hotfooted it over to Capitol Hill with a declaration that was short of war but that resulted in war anyway. I, along with 501 colleagues in the House and Senate, voted for the Tonkin Gulf resolution, which was Johnson's ticket to escalate our role in Vietnam.*
> Melvin R. Laird
> 2005

The 7th Fleet Admiral ordered the aircraft carrier *USS Constellation*, to join the carrier *Ticonderoga* and destroyers *Maddox* and *Turner Joy* in the Gulf of Tonkin. The base of operations for U.S. naval forces in the Gulf of Tonkin would henceforth be known for the next ten years as Yankee Station.

> *We cannot sit still as a nation and let them attack us*
> *on the high seas and get away with it.*
>
> Robert S. McNamara,
> Secretary of Defense
> August 1964

While President Johnson was broadcasting a message to a nation unsure of its role in a civil war 10,000 miles away, U.S. Navy fighter-bombers were en route from carriers on Yankee Station to attack targets in North Vietnam for the first time. These attacks would not be reported to the American people.

> *Repeated attacks of violence against the Armed Forces*
> *of the United States must be met, not only with alert*
> *defense, but with positive reply.*
>
> Lyndon B. Johnson,
> President of the United States
> Washington, DC,
> August 14, 1964, 11:37 p.m.

The President and Secretary of Defense had committed the country to war and the U.S. Congress had acceded to that request by approving the Gulf of Tonkin resolution. The buildup so accelerated through 1965 and 1966 that by 1967 the U.S. had 500,000 troops in Vietnam. Before the war was over, more than 2,700,000 American servicemen and women served in the war, and many thousands more supported the effort. The war claimed 58,000 American dead and 385,000 wounded in America's longest military conflict.

> *North Vietnam, over the course of the war, lost 1.1 million soldiers and*
> *2 million civilians, and yet they were willing to fight on and we were*
> *not. Victory meant everything to North Vietnam and nothing to the*
> *average American.*
>
> Melvin R. Laird
> 2005

INTRODUCTION

*When once you have tasted flight, you will forever walk the earth
with your eyes turned skyward, for there you have been
and there you will always long to return.*
                                        Leonardo da Vinci

I have been fascinated by flight for as long as I can remember. I'm not sure what triggered it—perhaps it was the first time I saw a crop-duster skimming just above the fields near my family's farm or saw a single engine biplane offering rides at the county fair—I just knew that something awesome was going on up there. As a child I could only dream of what it was, but being a dreamer I believed in my heart that somehow, some day, I would experience the thrill of flight. This dream remained a potent one throughout my adolescence, but by the time I was a young adult in the late 1950s and early 1960s, I was consumed by the intense pressures of college and medical school, with little opportunity to consider other interests.

When I entered military service in 1963, there was no question in my mind which branch of service I would choose. The United Stares Air Force offered everything I wanted; I could continue practicing medicine, have a chance to fly, and experience a vast world beyond the rural Midwest. The entry of the United States into the Vietnam Conflict was so gradual that it went almost unnoticed by young men my age, and I gave it nary a thought as I joined the Air Force. However, at the end of my service, I barely passed a day without thinking of the pilots and the events of the war that I knew there. The bravery they exhibited and the losses they endured seared into my consciousness, provoking both admiration and profound sadness. These emotions remain with me to this day.

The stories you are about to read are very personal. They chronicle the early years of the air war in Vietnam told from my perspective as a flight surgeon as well as from the perspective of several F-105 fighter pilots. I served in the United States Air Force from 1963 to 1966 and witnessed the unfolding involvement of our nation in the war. When I enlisted, Vietnam was not front-page news. Indeed, the news media either gave it no attention at all or buried it among clips of breaking news from around the world, including the war in the Congo, developments in Communist China, or the latest information on the Cold War with the Soviet

Union. In less than a year, however, the determined escalation of U.S. involvement in Southeast Asia changed everyone's perspective, and Vietnam became front-page headline news and the lead story on the evening news as reported by Walter Cronkite, Chet Huntley, David Brinkley, and others. The war became very familiar to all Americans.

There are a handful of sentinel dates from the air war in Vietnam—the Gulf of Tonkin incident in August 1964, which initiated the first air strikes into North Vietnam; the start of Operation Rolling Thunder in February 1965, which ordered bombing of selected targets in the North; and Operation Linebacker in December 1972, which brought B-52 heavy bombers to attack targets in-and-around Hanoi.

But for me, and the pilots I knew, the critical turning point of the war occurred on July 27, 1965—the first sorties of Operation Iron Hand. This tragic date is not well known to the public, or to historians, but for us it marked the end of the beginning and the beginning of the end.

My purpose in writing this book is to capture the profound importance of that day through the words of the pilots that flew the mission and through my perspective as a witness. I do not intend to provide a comprehensive analysis of the air war, a critique of its execution, or even a strictly biographical account of my time there. Instead, I hope to convey a sense of what it was like to be stationed in Southeast Asia during these early years of the war, what the pilots experienced during their missions, and what some of them endured as POWs.

In retrospect, it is very easy to be judgmental of our government's execution of the war, as directed by the President of the United States, Lyndon B. Johnson, and the Secretary of Defense, Robert L. McNamara. To those of us who were there in the early phase of the war, it became obvious, even prospectively, that the United States was sacrificing pilots, airplanes, and the opportunity for strategic air superiority in North Vietnam for political reasons—namely, to avoid a direct confrontation with the Soviet Union or China—while at the same time anticipating victory or a negotiated settlement in South Vietnam.

Russian-made MiG (Soviet-built Mikoyan-Gurevich) fighter planes sat on North Vietnamese runways and could not be bombed; antiaircraft artillery gunboats could not be sunk; Haiphong Harbor, a major entry-point of war materials from China and Russia, could not be blockaded or mined; and the capital city of Hanoi was surrounded by a 30-mile no-fly zone imposed by the Department of Defense and the White House. The penalty for any indiscretion of the rules was a court-martial. This was a phony war waged by the U.S. air warriors with one hand tied behind their back.

Yes, the Vietnam War was our war. It is our memory, and for many of us, it is our legacy. I am humbled and honored to have served with the dedicated pilots who faced daily danger in the skies over North Vietnam. I honor those who suffered confinement and torture as POWs, and above all, I honor those who made the supreme sacrifice for our country.

I
PEACETIME INNOCENCE—
FIRST ENCOUNTERS
1960 - 1964

U S STANDARD
ATMOSPHERIC
PRESSURE
TABLE

USAF AEROSPACE MEDICAL CENTER
BROOKS AFB TEXAS

AFPS SA APR 60, 5000

TYPHUS 1 YR

DATE OF EACH DOSE	AMOUNT	SIGNATURE, GRADE, AND SERVICE OF MEDICAL OFFICER
15 Mar 63	0.5cc	
12 Apr 63	0.5cc	
14 SEP 1964		
14 SEP 1965		

PLAGUE - 4 mo   FLU - 1 YR

OTHER IMMUNIZATIONS

DATE	LCT NO.	ANT.	MEDICAL OFFICER
9 JUL 1964	CHIK #1		I.S.C.
22 Oct '63	FLU		K. Lewis CAPT USAF
OCT 1964	SABIN II		M.b.K
2 APR 1965	Plague G-8834	0.5c	CH Bramlett
12 May 1965	Flu	0.5c	R.H. Bonner
28 MAY 1965	Plague #2 G-8987	0.2	C.B. Marshall
8 Nov 65	Flu	1cc	R.H. Bonner
10 Dec 65	Plague G-8990	0.2	R.H. Bonner

SENSITIVITY TESTS (Tuberculin, Schick, etc.)

DATE	TYPE	DOSE	ROUTE	RESULT	MED. OFF.
12 Sept 63	TB Fine			Neg	
14 Mar 66	TB Fine			Neg	

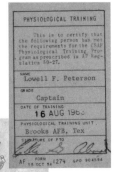

UNITED STATES OF AMERICA
DEPARTMENT OF DEFENSE

CERTIFICAT DE VACCINATION

DÉLIVRÉ CONFORMÉMENT À L'ARTICLE 99 DU RÈGLEMENT SANITAIRE INTERNATIONAL

IMMUNIZATION CERTIFICATE

ISSUED IN ACCORDANCE WITH ARTICLE 99 INTERNATIONAL SANITARY REGULATIONS

MEDICAL SERVICES
CERTIFIED IMMUNIZATION

LAST NAME—FIRST NAME—MIDDLE NAME
Peterson, Lowell Frank

SERVICE NO.	DEPARTMENT
AO3126846	USAF

DATE OF BIRTH	RACE	SEX
26 May 1936	Cauc	M

SIGNATURE OF ABOVE PERSON
Lowell F. Peterson

REMARKS (Drug, Foreign Protein or Serum Sensitivity, etc.)

Blood type — AB +

Sensitive — Horse Serum

ARMED FORCES OF THE UNITED STATES

CAPTAIN   INDEFINITE

Lowell F. Peterson   FV3126846

PROPERTY OF THE UNITED STATES GOVERNMENT

ARMED FORCES OF THE UNITED STATES

GENEVA CONVENTIONS IDENTIFICATION CARD

NOT A PASS

This card is issued in accordance with the provisions of the Geneva Conventions of August 12, 1949. (May to be used for other identification.)

LAST NAME - FIRST NAME - MIDDLE NAME	GRADE
PETERSON, LOWELL F	CAPT

BRANCH OF SERVICE	SERVICE NUMBER	DATE OF BIRTH
USAF	AO3126848	26May36

IF FOUND, DROP IN NEAREST U. S. MAIL BOX

PHYSIOLOGICAL TRAINING

This is to certify that the following person has met the requirements for the USAF Physiological Training Program as prescribed in AF Regulation 50-27.

NAME
Lowell F. Peterson

GRADE
Captain

DATE OF TRAINING
16 AUG 196

PHYSIOLOGICAL TRAINING UNIT
Brooks AFB, Tex

SIGNATURE OF PTO

AF FORM 1274   15 OCT 54   GPO 904594

UNITED STATES AIR FORCE

SCHOOL OF AEROSPACE MEDICINE

AIR FORCE SYSTEMS COMMAND

Be it known _____ CAPTAIN LOWELL F. PETERSON _____ is a graduate of

PRIMARY COURSE IN AEROSPACE MEDICINE

In testimony whereof, and by authority vested in us, we do confer this diploma. Given at Brooks Air Force Base, Texas. This 20th Day of September 19 63

Harold V. Ellingson
COLONEL, USAF, MC
COMMANDER SCHOOL OF AEROSPACE MEDICINE

T. C. Bedwell, Jr.
MAJOR GENERAL, USAF, MC
COMMANDER AEROSPACE MEDICAL DIVISION

John V. Baceman
COURSE SUPERVISOR

Ferdinand Barnum
LT. COLONEL, USAF, MC
DIRECTOR OF EDUCATION

Enlistment

Not many people know about Dr. Frank Berry, but he was responsible for the enlistment choices of some 26,000 doctors, including myself. In 1954 Dr. Frank Berry was appointed as Assistant Secretary of Defense for Medical Affairs. He introduced the Berry Plan, a proposal to allow young physicians the choice of three service options when they entered the draft. Doctors could enter the armed forces immediately after their internship before entering specialty residency training or private practice; they could enter two years after medical school and return to their practice or complete their residency after service; or, they could enter the service after their residency training.

I entered the military after my medical internship, and since the Air Force was the only choice I wanted to consider, I immediately completed an application for flight surgeon school. In the spring of 1963, I received a call at Milwaukee Lutheran Hospital from my wife.

"Your orders came," she told me. "You are to report to Brooks Air Force Base, San Antonio, Texas, by July 6th for flight surgeon school."

The orders went on to say that I would be assigned to Kadena Air Force Base, Okinawa, in October.

"It says here that accompanied tours of duty with dependents into a foreign theater requires a three-year commitment," she said. "I guess, if you want to fly and you want overseas duty, you better take it."

If I had waited to be drafted into the army, and was stationed in the United States, or took an unaccompanied tour overseas, my service obligation would have been 18 months.

I arrived at Brooks Air Force Base, San Antonio, Texas, for flight surgeon school in early July. The temperature was a stifling 90 degrees by eight o'clock in the morning. Luckily, my wife and I found an apartment complex with a swimming pool and air-conditioning near Fort Sam Houston, a large army training base.

Three other flight surgeon recruits lived there as well, which allowed us to carpool to Brooks each day for classes. Driving through Fort Sam, we were religiously saluted by the new army recruits who had probably been instructed to salute anything that moved. We were all captains and initially accepted their gestures graciously. However, after a few days we began rotating the occupant of the right front seat, who responded for all of us as our designated saluter.

At the base I learned the proper way to wear a uniform and memorized the rules of military etiquette. I also learned not to carry my briefcase, or anything for that matter, in my right hand. One day while walking to class with my head down to avoid the sun's scorching reflection from the white sidewalk, I looked up to see a sergeant saluting me. With my right hand full, by reflex, I responded with a left-hand salute. The sergeant could barely control himself from laughing, although I did hear a chuckle as we passed.

The classroom work was not exactly what doctors were accustomed to. We learned about oxygen masks and regulators instead of anatomy and physiology. We went to decompression chambers instead of surgical suites, and ejection seat training replaced emergency rooms and trauma centers. We also watched movies about Air Force history and about flying, and, of course, we learned how to complete medical flight physical forms in triplicate.

At one point during our curriculum we were taken to Randolph Air Force Base for a flight in a T-33 jet trainer, which was a real thrill. The pilot allowed me to fly the plane for a while, and I think I did an acceptable job of keeping it straight and level. He instructed me on making aileron rolls, which I did. He then asked me if there was anything else that I would like to do. I said that I would like to experience what it was like to pull some G-force (gravity pull). A few tight 3-G turns later without the benefit of an inflatable G-suit to compress my lower body, I was ready to call it a day. Returning to Randolph, my flight suit soaked with sweat and a bit nauseous, I was still able to recover without embarrassment. Thereafter, I was much more appreciative of what pilots routinely experience.

Graduation day came in early October 1963. Although it was a very familiar ceremony, with the pageantry, speeches, and presentation of diplomas similar to high school, college, and medical school graduations, somehow it was different. The ceremony opened with the Pledge of Allegiance and concluded with the "Star Spangled Banner." The recessional march from the auditorium, accompanied by the "Air Force Hymn," made chills run down my spine. At that moment, I felt proud to be a part of the United States Air Force.

The Birds Were Silver Then

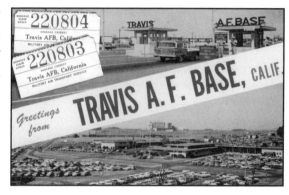

The butterflies of fear and anxiety were in mortal combat with the excitement I felt as I left Travis Air Force Base (AFB), California, en route to Kadena AFB, Okinawa. The flight along the Canadian Pacific Coast toward our first stop in Anchorage, Alaska, was serene, with the bright moonlight reflecting off the snow-capped mountains. Anchorage was stunningly quiet, with only the slow movements of the ground crew servicing our plane in the sub-zero cold disturbing the stillness.

As we landed at Tokyo International Airport eleven hours later at 0200 local time, I realized I had passed through ten time zones and gained a whole day by crossing the International Dateline in less than twenty-four hours. Looking through the airplane window I saw numerous neon signs, all written in Japanese.

I suddenly felt lonesome for home, a little bit depressed, and a lot more scared. What had I gotten myself into? As we took off from Tokyo, I was glad to see those neon signs recede into the distance. At the same time, I knew the isolation I felt would not completely disappear.

We finally touched down at Kadena AFB, Okinawa, about five hours later than our scheduled time of arrival. Wearing my dress-blue uniform, garrison cap, a stubbly beard, and twenty-four hours of BO, I left the calm interior of the 707 and stepped into pure chaos.

As I stood outside the terminal at Base Operations, I heard a soft voice ask, "Are you Dr. Peterson?" A colonel's wife who had volunteered to meet new arrivals, even at 0400 hours, was standing in front of me. After I answered in the affirmative, she said, "Follow me; Dr. Levin is waiting for you inside." She introduced me to Dr. Ken Levin in the coffee shop and then she went off in search of more bewildered souls.

Captain Levin had volunteered to meet my plane on this early Sunday morning and transport me to the Base Officer's Quarters (BOQ). We chatted over a cup of coffee until my luggage was unloaded, and then we headed for his car. This was to be another adventure. Captain Levin had an old "Henry J.", a Kaiser automobile, that was mostly rusted out—so much so, that I could see the concrete passing by below my feet through the floorboards. I was soon to learn that the salty ocean mist constantly in the air over the island was disastrous to cars.

The trip from Kadena Base Operations to the BOQ was a short mile on streets that wound through the center of Kadena Air Force Base, traversing past the runways, taxiways, and hangars. A short distance from Base Ops, Ken pulled off to the side of the road to point out one of the most incredible sites I was to experience in my whole Air Force career.

To my left, stood the flightline (concrete airplane ramp), lit up like a college football stadium. Huge generators emitted a high-pitched whine; it was a song that I would hear nightly for the next three years.

"Well, there they are," Ken said, pointing to the long row of F-105 aircraft. "The last ones just arrived this week. All of the F-100s have gone back to the States. You'll get well acquainted with the jocks who fly them, I'm sure."

I would learn later that the F-105 Thunderchief is the only airplane that has ever been exclusively a United States Air Force (USAF) airplane. It was never used by another service, and it was never sold or exported to another country. It would fly more sorties against North Vietnam than any other aircraft. The airplane, affectionately nicknamed the "Thud", was designed as an all-weather fighter-bomber. Its J75-

F-105D with an open drag chute

P-19W Pratt and Whitney engine is capable of producing 26,500 pounds of thrust in afterburner mode. The average cruising speed is 507 knots with combat speed up to 726 knots. Maximum rate of climb is 35,000 feet per minute.

> *An F-105 accelerating in afterburner on the deck in smooth air was a breathtaking experience, which ranked somewhere between sex and a good drag-chute on a short runway.*
>
> Brig. Gen. Ken Bell, USAF (Ret.)
> 2000

The F-105D can carry 750 or 1,000 pound bombs, bullpup missiles, sidewinder missiles, two pods of rocket launchers with 19 rockets each, and it can carry nuclear weapons. Its M-61, six-barrel, 20mm cannon has 1,028 rounds of ammunition, capable of firing at a rate of 6,000 rounds per minute.

F-105 with six 650-pound bombs underneath and bullpups and a sidewinder outboard

The F-105 was the most honest, comfortable, and stable aircraft to fly. The radar bombing system and the 20mm Gatling gun were great. When the pipper and little green squiggly (bomb or gun-sight indicators) were both on the target, you could expect a hit when you pulled the trigger.
Col. Paul Craw, USAF (Ret.)
2005

F-105 takes the runway

As I looked at the flightline, I could not remember ever being so impressed by anything in my life. One hundred brand-spanking-new F-105 fighter planes were lined up, perfectly parked, side-by-side, at a slight angle to ninety-degrees. Their pure silver skin shone and reflected the spotlights just as the Alaskan snow-covered mountains had reflected the moonlight. The numbers, USAF decals, and U.S. flags painted on the tails; the black nosecones; the clear plexiglas canopies, all in the raised position, were majestic. But, nothing was as distracting as the glint of reflected light on the silver skin, stretched tight over the fuselages of one-hundred airplanes all the way to the horizon.

We sat there a full ten minutes. I was in awe, and I don't think I said a word. Then, we drove on to the BOQ in the contrasting mobile relic of the old Henry J. in silence. I had been introduced to the birds when they were silver! All of a sudden I was not tired, confused, homesick, or anything else—I was excited! For the first time, I knew I had made the right decision. My destiny was to be a part of this adventure, wherever it took me. At that point, I could not have possibly imagined what lie ahead.

My First Day

I finally arrived at my Base Officer's Quarters (BOQ) room at 0500 local time. In spite of catching very little sleep during the 24-hour flight, I couldn't rest. My brain was still on Central Daylight Time, and according to my biological clock, it was 1400 hours the previous day. I reasoned that I might as well turn on the radio, lie back, and hope to doze off. I flicked on the radio and heard a familiar voice—well, almost familiar. It was the Lone Ranger—in Japanese! Tonto in Japanese sounded like a Samurai warrior, but at least I could understand "Kemosabe".

As I lay on my cot in this reinforced concrete building, one of more than a dozen identical structures that lined the main road through the air base, I was suddenly jolted out of bed by the loudspeakers all over the base, shouting—"Typhoon condition four! Typhoon condition four! Typhoon condition four!" I jumped up and looked out the window. Nothing was moving. It was a dead landscape. I did not know what to do. Was I supposed to go to a shelter? Should I report to my duty station, wherever it was? Not seeing anyone else, I decided to do nothing. I found out later that "typhoon condition four" means that the typhoon is two hundred-fifty miles away. No one gets nervous about a direct hit on the island until condition two, which means it could strike within twenty-four hours. I was to learn that when condition two arrives, the airplanes evacuate to Korea. Also, everyone leaves their duty stations and returns home to duct tape their windows, and stock up on food, batteries, flashlights, candles, beer, and soda at the commissary. The pre-typhoon parties during condition two consume most of the alcohol on the base and the shelves of the commissary go bare in hours. During condition one—which my wife and daughter would experience in 1965—the one-hundred-mile per hour winds flood the houses by driving a deluge of horizontal rain right under doors and window sashes. Electricity is lost and water for bathing and flushing toilets comes from previously filled bathtubs and buckets. (Washing and drying cloth diapers—the only kind available—under these conditions presented a challenge.)

I gave up on the radio program, put my trust in the reinforced concrete BOQ that reminded me more of a prison than an officer's quarters, and finally drifted off to sleep. A few hours later my sleep was interrupted by the entry of another new arrival, Bob Kasabian, a dentist, who became my roommate in "the jail".

On Sunday afternoon, my first day at Kadena Air Force Base, Ken Levin returned, along with his friend and fellow general medical officer, Ed Doyle, to take me to lunch at the Kadena Officers Club. I was impressed by how the Okinawan waitresses responded to our every demand. All we had to say was, *naisan*, and they were right there. I was disturbed to learn later that *naisan* was not necessarily a particularly endearing title (slave?).

We spent the afternoon touring the island and visited Dan and Pat McAllen. Dan was the executive officer at the medical dispensary and I would soon get to know him as a friend. He was promoted to Major later during my tour of duty, and was on his way to a nice Air Force career, only to have it blown away (literally) by a ruptured aneurysm in his brain. Death was instantaneous. The loss of this good man left a sadness in the hearts of all who knew him.

Later, on that Sunday afternoon we gravitated to the Officers Club for a ritual called "French-75s". I was warned ahead of time to go easy on these drinks—a concoction of powdered sugar, gin, and champagne in a Tom Collins glass—as they were known to jump up and bite you. The whole scene reminded me of when I was a freshman medical student drinking punch made from 100-proof lab alcohol stolen from the anatomy lab. The alcohol was designed to "pickle you", whether you were dead or alive.

As I tasted my first French-75,

French-75
Officers Club
Kadena
Air Force Base,
Okinawa

8 servings

1 c water
1 c sugar
4 c ice cubes
1 c Bombay Sapphire gin or
        other premium gin, divided
1/2 c fresh lemon juice, divided
1 750-ml bottle champagne

Stir 1 c water and 1 c sugar in medium saucepan over medium heat until sugar dissolves; bring to a boil. Reduce heat, chill.
Chill 8 Tom Collins glasses 2 hours.
Place 1 c ice, 1/4 c gin, 2 T lemon juice, and 3 T simple syrup in cocktail shaker. Shake well, then strain into 2 chilled glasses. Repeat 3 more times to make 8 drinks total. Divide champagne among glasses and serve. •

I met Cliffe Laborde, a general medical officer from Louisiana, who had arrived one week earlier. We would become close friends. Cliffe had a week's advantage over me on how to deal with the 75s. He apparently had not fared well on his first encounter and was much more cautious on this Sunday. The bar at the club was jammed with couples, single officers, male and female, and guys like Cliffe and me, who were awaiting our wives' arrival a month or six weeks later.

After a couple of hours, we stumbled into the dining room for dinner before going off to our beds to rest and let the toxins metabolize. Still being on Wisconsin time, however, I was wide awake, if not totally lucid. I wandered off-base to investigate the night spots in Koza City.

What I encountered was amazing. Neon signs sporting names like: Playboy Club, Ecstacy, Las Vegas, Paris Revue, and Hollywood East enticed the U.S. troops to spend their time and their money. There were B-girls hustling drinks and looking for companions, bands playing off-key, and native Okinawan girls singing English words to popular American songs that they neither understood nor could put into context. Cheap Scotch was poured from a refilled Johnnie Walker bottle. After a few hours of soaking up the sights and the libations, I finally decided that I would be able to sleep. I hailed a *skoshi* (small) cab and returned to Gate I at Kadena Air Base. I was surprised, but thankful, that the Air Police let me back on the base. As I lay down in my bed and felt it start to spin, I couldn't help but think about home and how far away it really was.

Black Matt

It was the evening of my first time on duty as the MOD (Medical Officer of the Day) at the Kadena Air Force Dispensary (medical clinic) when I received a call that there had been an aircraft accident, and that I was to prepare for treatment of a possible casualty. I had been on Okinawa only a short time and was just getting oriented to the routine of treating air force personnel and their dependents. Callous as it may sound, I was happy for the emergency, as it got the dependents out of the dispensary and let me focus on a true emergency.

Capt. James W. Matthews

The reports were sketchy, but I was advised an F-105 had crashed in the East China Sea. The pilot had ejected successfully, but his condition was unknown. Within an hour, while we monitored the rescue and return-to-base of the ejected pilot, I tried to recall what I had learned at flight surgeon's school about evaluating, treating, and writing reports on victims of aircraft accidents. I soon decided that this was all academic without having the patient in front of me. After awhile, the entourage of wing commander, squadron commander, flight commander, executive officer, and the rescued pilot arrived at the clinic. I was impressed and a little bit intimidated.

The F-105s of the 67th Squadron had been out at the bombing range doing low-level skip-bombing and toss-bombing at targets when Maj. James "Black Matt" Matthews' airplane had a sudden catastrophic mechanical problem: the "stab-aug" (stabilization augmentation) on-board computer system, which was supposed to automatically keep the airplane stable on approach to the target malfunctioned, and the plane pitched straight up. Matt immediately recognized his aircraft was out of control and the problem was irreversible. He was now living in a very narrow envelope of time. In a split second, he blew his canopy, ejected, and was in the air only long enough to get an open chute.

When he arrived at the Kadena dispensary, I was relieved he was alive and without major bodily injury. However, he had the most severe back and neck muscle spasms I had ever seen. It was as if he was mummified. The violent pitch of the plane traveling at 0.9 MACH (1.0 MACH=speed of sound=approximately 660 knots or 760 mph at altitude), had triggered every muscle in his upper body to assume the consistency of a bowstring.

After examining Matt, I gave him a shot of morphine and a muscle relaxant, which, in time, began to ease his discomfort.

I was ready to send him home with instructions for hot baths and massage when Matt looked at me, and said, "Doc, you're not going to ground me are you?"

I deferred. "Matt, come back here tomorrow morning. We'll see how you feel. Oh, by the way, Chivas Regal and Jack Daniels are great muscle relaxants, but don't spread the word that I said that."

Matt said, "Doc, the Air Force has been good to me. Flying is the only thing I know how to do. I do it well, and I'm thankful for the opportunity. If I die doing my job in this Air Force toy, I won't blame anyone, but you can bet that I will give one hundred-and-ten percent every time I crawl into that cockpit."

As he left, I couldn't help but be amazed at his attitude and thought to myself, "Matt Matthews is a class act!"

Matt Matthews had a distinguished career in the Air Force. He assumed command of the 67th Squadron following the shoot down and capture of Col. Robinson Risner. He retired as a full Colonel. I was saddened to learn that Matt died suddenly a few years ago. But, I'm sure he was thankful to the end that on that day long ago his plane chose to pitch up instead of down.

Unexpected Delays

I had arrived at Kadena in late October 1963, but did not get orders placing me on flying status until November. I was then required to accrue four hours of flying time each month. However, as a flight surgeon I was encouraged to accompany aircrews on flights as often as possible so that I could better understand their lifestyle and their medical concerns.

In the early 1960s, Lieut. Col. William "Bill" Mitchell was in charge of the Military Air Transport Service (MATS) unit, which would later be renamed Military Airlift Command (MAC). Colonel Mitchell had served in World War II and Korea, and had probably seen more hours in the air than most people. He was mild-mannered, rosey-cheeked, and had snow-white hair. He ran his unit in an efficient military manner. He occasionally flew C-54s out of Base Flight for his required flying time as a command pilot, and would nightly stop at the Officers Club stag bar to drink two Gibson's-on-the-rocks before retiring to his home in the officers' housing area.

Colonel Mitchell, along with Maj. Joe Banks at Base Flight Operations, were the number one contacts for flight surgeons needing to hitch a ride somewhere to get flying time. I had been told early on in my tour of duty by the senior flight surgeons that it was my job, along with theirs, to keep Colonel Mitchell flying, otherwise our ability to get trips anywhere in the Far East would be jeopardized. Don't get me wrong. Colonel Mitchell was a very good pilot and when he presented himself for his annual flight physical, I signed his papers as eligible, slight Gibson tremor and all. If I had identified any serious medical problems, I would have been true to my medical oaths and grounded him, but it seemed prudent and ethical to overlook a few minor flaws related to age.

My first flight arranged by Colonel Mitchell was supposed to be an overnight flight to Clark Air Base in the Philippines on a C-124 cargo plane, better known as "Old Shaky". I naïvely arrived for the trip in full dress blue uniform as I had been erroneously instructed to do at flight surgeon's school. The crew, comfortable in their flight suits, chuckled, but welcomed me aboard and did not tease me too much about my rookie mistake. During the flight, we encountered a tremendous storm with a lot of turbulence, which may have accounted for our subsequent mechanical problems. I was instructed by the crew to lie in one of the canvas bunks and hang on. I did hang on—tight—to the metal frame as the storm continued to buffet our airplane for 30 minutes or more. I remember being thrown two feet into the air and then slammed down hard onto the canvas like a loser in a heavyweight fight.

After we landed at Clark Field, the pilot told me, "Yup, that was a bad one; that kind of storm can flip you upside down and that would have been curtains for us!"

When I arrived in the Philippines, I realized how close to the equator I was. Even though it was January, the air was stifling hot, a situation made even more

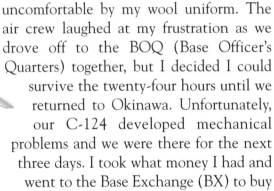

C-124

uncomfortable by my wool uniform. The air crew laughed at my frustration as we drove off to the BOQ (Base Officer's Quarters) together, but I decided I could survive the twenty-four hours until we returned to Okinawa. Unfortunately, our C-124 developed mechanical problems and we were there for the next three days. I took what money I had and went to the Base Exchange (BX) to buy

a pair of slacks, a light shirt, and a change of underwear. This, of course, left me with barely enough money to eat and certainly not enough to drink. So, for the next three days I was stuck in the stinking, steaming BOQ with only a paperback Western for diversion. On the positive side, I had learned a valuable lesson: never assume anything. Always bring enough clothes and money to sustain yourself for an extended period of time.

In February 1964, Colonel Mitchell arranged a flight for me to Bangkok, Thailand, on a C-130 cargo plane. This time, I was a lot smarter. I wore my flight suit, packed some slacks, light shirts, and underwear to last several days, and took enough money to last a week. The flight crew was again very accommodating and friendly and I had a nice conversation with multiple crew members during the long eight-hour flight to Don Muong Airport in Bangkok. As we were flying into Bangkok, a propeller mechanically malfunctioned and had to be "feathered", which means the engine was shut down and the propeller blades were frozen in a position cutting directly into the wind to avoid the drag-resistance that would occur if they were left perpendicular to the direction of flight. Our captain contacted the local U.S. Air Force liaison group, and with their help, sent Twix (telegraphic) messages to Clark Air Force Base, Kadena Air Force Base, Tachikawa Air Force Base, Fifth Air Force headquarters in Tokyo, and eventually all the way back to bases in the States looking for a new propeller. Unfortunately, it soon became apparent that no propeller would be forthcoming from any of these locations at least until the following week, at the earliest. Once again I was stuck, but at least this time I had appropriate clothes and some extra money. No one could have possibly believed at that time, just over one year later, the United States would be deeply involved in the Vietnam War and that an endless supply of airplane parts and propellers would be readily available in Southeast Asia within hours.

On this occasion, however, our crew had no choice but to go to the Grand Hotel in downtown Bangkok and wait it out. The first night there, being rather tired from the trip, the crew and I had a light dinner in the hotel dining area and went to bed. The next day, I walked the streets in my civilian clothes

C-130

like any other tourist, and rode from site to site in a three-wheeled propane-gas-propelled taxi for a few Baht (Thai dollars). The Reclining Buddha, the Emerald Buddha, the Temple of the Dawn, the Royal Palace, and of course, the lapidaries and Thai silk stores made for an interesting day. That evening, after a spicy stir-fried dinner, I wandered into the hotel bar and ordered a Singha beer.

It was a dreary bar, in an equally dreary hotel, on the fringe of downtown Bangkok. It was incredibly humid—the walls literally dripping with sweat. The ceiling fans and the cross-ventilated full-length open windows did little to dispel the stifling heat, which was oppressive for this non-native. The Thai bartender, with his sparkling almond eyes, straight black hair, and easy smile, delighted his customers by snapping the caps off the Singha bottles with great flourish. The lone television set above the back bar gleefully flickered with the night's entertainment, a violent kick-boxing match, excitedly described by the Thai announcer, who only became less animated when he delivered a requiem for the loser of the match: *"Mai pen lai"* (it doesn't matter). The bartender moved idly back and forth, urging on his favorite boxer. Mercifully, after hundreds of kicks and punches to the head and body, the matches ended and the bartender disconsolately settled onto his barstool under a ceiling fan at the far end of the bar, as a program of classical Thai dancing came on

Bangkok, 1964

the TV. The graceful movements of the beautiful Thai girls was much more to my liking.

I had missed his entry, probably in a moment of deep thoughtfulness or inattention, but I soon became aware of another westerner at the bar, sipping Singha. He was younger than I—muscled, blond, blue-eyed, hair cut short, football build, coordinated in his movements, confident in his bearing.

I decided to strike up a conversation and asked him if he was an American. He said he was. It appeared that he was anxious to talk, and I ordered up another Singha beer for each of us. I asked him why he was in Bangkok, because, in my day's excursion I had seen no other Americans. He informed me that he was on R&R (rest and relaxation) from Vietnam. This utterly amazed me. We only had a few hundred advisers in Vietnam at the time, so I asked him what his role was. He stated that he was a pilot flying observation flights as a forward-air-controller (FAC) in a small O-1E Cessna airplane. He would fly over the battlefields looking for concentrations of Viet Cong and then radio the position to the South Vietnamese Air Force headquarters, which would send airplanes to bomb the Viet Cong enclave. As the observer, he would drop colored smoke flares in the area where he had spotted troop movement. The Vietnamese planes were mostly old propeller driven training aircraft that had been rigged to carry a few bombs. I asked him how good the Vietnam Air Force pilots were. He flashed a sardonic smile and gave a small chuckle, describing the Vietnamese pilots as less than courageous. He said they often dropped their bombs well away from the area he had marked, to avoid being shot at by ground fire. If anyone did shoot at them, they left the area as quickly as possible. He said that occasionally U.S. Air Force advisors would fly with the Vietnamese pilots trying to instruct them in the appropriate combat and bombing techniques, but even then, the pilots would still not carry out their mission. In his opinion there was no way the South Vietnamese Republican forces could defeat the Viet Cong alone.

Cessna 0-1 "Bird Dog" U.S. Air Force forward-air controller (FAC)

We talked further over a couple more Singhas and this young man became less and less engaged. I suspect the thought of returning to South Vietnam played on his mind. I began to feel less talkative myself. The air felt like a sodden blanket on my skin and I started getting a headache, as if the tarnish colonizing every piece of metal in the place was starting to blacken my gray matter. Chalking it up to dehydration, I said goodbye to the pilot, wished him well, and went off to bed.

After five days in Bangkok, with still no sign of a propeller, my money exhausted, and my temporary-duty orders nearly outdated, I found a flight on a General's airplane to Taiwan, and then with some smooth talking and my military orders, I finagled my way onto a commercial Southern Air Transport flight to Kadena. Once I returned home, I could easily claim that my trip to Bangkok was a relatively short digression without any significance, but in my heart, I knew how fast things were moving in our Vietnam involvement, and how much I had learned during this short trip.

Operation Air Boon Choo at Camp Nasty

On April 3, 1964, I received orders for deployment on temporary duty assignment (TDY) from Kadena AFB, Okinawa, to Korat Royal Thai AFB, Thailand, in support of a Southeast Asia Treaty Organization (SEATO) war games exercise, Operation Air Boon Choo. As luck would have it, I boarded the C-130 in Okinawa with a bad case of stomach flu. Knowing the cargo plane had no bathroom, I settled into the eight-hour flight praying that I would make it through without incident. I slept most of the way, feverish, dehydrated, and oblivious to the noise.

The official dates of the exercise were April 20-30, 1964, but the mobilization went on for weeks ahead of time. By the time I arrived at Korat, the Royal Thai Air Base was already teeming with military vehicles, road graders, bulldozers, large communication dishes, and generators.

REQUEST AND AUTHORIZATION FOR TEMPORARY DUTY TRAVEL OF MILITARY PERSONNEL		DATE 3 April 1964
(If more space is required, continue on reverse, identifying items by number.)		

I. REQUEST FOR AUTHORIZATION	
TO: Chief Administrative Services, Hq 6313 AB Wg FROM: *(Requesting authority)* Detachment 4, 1st Medical Service Wing	1. REQUEST TDY BE AUTHORIZED AS INDICATED IN ITEMS 5 THROUGH 12
2. TYPED NAME, GRADE AND TITLE OF AUTHORIZED OFFICIAL WALTER C. KUROWSKI Lt Col, USAF Director of Personnel	3. SIGNATURE OF AUTHORIZED OFFICIAL *Walter C. Kurowski*	4. PHONE NR. 42160

II. TEMPORARY DUTY TRAVEL ORDERS

5. THE FOLLOWING INDIVIDUAL(S) WILL PROCEED AS INDICATED. UPON COMPLETION WILL RETURN TO PROPER STATION.

GRADE	NAME *(First name, middle initial, last name, AFSN)*	ORGANIZATION	SECURITY CLEARANCE FOR PERIOD OF TDY
CAPTAIN	LOWELL F. PETERSON, AO3126846, AFSC 9356	Det 4, 1st Med Svc Wg	SECRET
TSGT	RONALD D. NICKOLETT, AF27873592, AFSC 90170	Det 4, 1st Med Svc Wg	SECRET
SSGT	LEONARD F. FULLERTON, AF12454825, AFSC 90270B	Det 4, 1st Med Svc Wg	SECRET
A2C	GEORGE E. PORTIS, AF14811533, AFSC 90650	Det 4, 1st Med Svc Wg	SECRET

///

6. DEPART ON OR ABOUT 10 April 1964	7. APPROXIMATE NR. OF DAYS *(Include travel time)* 24	8. DDALV

As I exited the C-130 at Korat, I was met by a welcoming committee consisting of Captain Clark, the base commander, a Hawaiian second lieutenant who was to command the Air Police during the exercise, and two lieutenants from Tachikawa AFB, near Tokyo, who were serving as executive and personnel officers. The senior non-commissioned officer, Senior Master Sergeant Yaxzyn, a lovable, rotund fellow with thick glasses was also there and quickly took charge of my orientation to the base. Although Captain Clark was in command of the Air Force compound, a colonel from Kadena AFB assumed command for the duration of the exercise. It just wouldn't look right to have a captain in charge of a base now teeming with majors, lieutenant colonels, colonels, and generals.

Korat Air Base in the spring of 1964 was a pretty bleak place. Located on a high plain in central Thailand, the surrounding landscape consisted of sagebrush and sand broken up by an occasional group of low trees. However, the base did have a very adequate, 10,000-foot-long concrete runway, which the Thai Air Force used for training purposes. Sergeant Yaxzyn and his lieutenants had nicknamed the base, "Camp Nasty" after a mangy, cachectic, mutt irreverently called "Nasty" that scrounged through the garbage behind the mess hall.

The compound was made up of hooches (wooden barracks), each able to house eight cots. The sides of the hooches were slatted boards over screening with drop-down thatch shutters. The floors were solid matched boards, perfect for keeping unwanted critters out, and the roofs were covered with steel. There was a communal shower building with a hot water boiler on the rooftop; a mess hall, which served non-coms as well as officers; and a six-by-six foot base exchange (BX) that sold shaving cream, toothpaste, razors, and other toiletries. I was given an entire hooch for my medical dispensary, which precluded a need to pitch our large tents in the arid boondocks.

I soon learned that the most annoying and persistent vermin in this area of the world were mosquitoes and rats. The screens helped with the former, but I also used mosquito netting over my bunk. After all, I was in an endemic malaria area and could not expect chloroquine drug prophylaxis to do everything. I also learned not to keep food in the hooch. If this principle was violated, my hooch-mates and I might find ourselves face-to-face with an ugly rat at 3 a.m. as it took care of our Hershey bars.

Shortly after arrival, I was informed the troops digging latrines out of the prairie surrounding the camp had killed four cobra snakes. My stomach flu disappeared the minute I heard that. There were raised boardwalk pathways from the hooches to the latrines. For the first few days, I never went anywhere, especially to the latrine at night, without a flashlight in hand and combat boots on my feet.

However, before long—cavalier, courageous, or stupid—I was walking to the latrine in shower clogs and my boxer shorts.

Along with cobras, Thailand is home to the extremely poisonous kraits, huge boa constrictors, and of course, scorpions. The urinals were out in the open areas near the hooches and consisted of a pipe driven in the sand with a funnel in the top. One night, an airman went out to the urinal in his shower clogs and as he stood relieving himself, he stepped on a scorpion. The critter in a reflexive defensive action, whipped its tail around and stung the unsuspecting airman on the ankle. It was a painful, but not particularly dangerous, wound that caused his foot to swell to double its size.

The Thai army provided security guards on the flightline and runways, and at night they all carried wooden clubs. One night a Thai guard stepped on a large constrictor snake, which had probably slithered up onto the warm runway for comfort. The snake began to curl around the guard, who then used his club to beat it to death. The snake was brought into camp the next day and created quite a stir, as airmen had their pictures taken with this nine-foot-long, six-inch-wide snake wrapped around their shoulders.

When the exercise got underway many complicated war games were being played, but I really was not involved until one fateful day when I was standing in the middle of the hooch compound. Without warning, a T-33 jet swooped down over me at fifty feet off the ground, momentarily scaring the crap out of me.

Moments later, one of the umpires for the exercise arrived and informed me, "Doc, you and your no-sweat pills (venereal disease prevention medication) have just been blasted all over the camp; you are out of the game."

I reacted to the news in true military fashion; I wrote up a full report of our medical mission and why it had been compromised, receiving in response oral commendations.

During the exercise, the air operations, the camp, and even our dispensary were inspected by Pameng Kantarat, the Air Vice Marshal of the Royal Thai Air Force, and by Maj. Gen. Albert P. Clark, Commander 313th Air Division. The King of Thailand also came for a motorized inspection tour and was the honored guest at the formal closing ceremonies of the exercise, as several flights of F-105s did a formation fly-over. Evidently, the King was dutifully impressed with the demonstration and pageantry, because less than a year later, the United States Air Force commenced combat operations over North Vietnam from bases in Thailand.

During the exercise, the combined Airmens, Non-Commissioned Officers (NCOs), and Officers Club at Korat, was a single hooch where cold beer was sold in the very hot late afternoon and evening. I remember sitting at the club with

Col. Lawrence "Dagwood" Damewood, Col. Grant "Grunt" Smith, and Col. Floyd "Buckshot" White, when a flight of F-105s flew over the base at supersonic speed. The shock of the sound barrier-breaking-waves hitting this hooch was like an explosion—the timbers vibrating and the walls barely resisting collapse. All three colonels vaulted out of their chairs into the compound trying to get tail numbers of the airplanes that had committed transgression of the rules. It was a laughable experience, especially watching those colonels spill their beer as they tore out of the hooch into the late afternoon sun.

In the end, Operation Air Boon Choo was a success and I was thrilled to have been a part of it, but I was also anxious to return home. My firstborn child, Linda Ruth, would be born just one month later at Camp Kue Army Hospital on Okinawa. Little did I know then, that in another year, I would be back at Camp Nasty, but this time the war would not be a game. It would be real.

II
COMBAT DEPLOYMENT—
AUGUST 1964 - JUNE 1965
IN THEIR OWN WORDS

Vietnam was a crisis of the American identity.
It was often said that Americans lost
their innocence there, which, if true,
may not have been an altogether bad thing.
Innocence allied to great power may be refreshing
but can be very dangerous.

Lance Morrow
Time
April 15, 1985

F-105s deploying to Southeast Asia

Battle Damage

by
Jim Sandin, First Lieutenant
Kilo Flight, 12th Tactical Fighter Squadron

In November 1964, I was sent on temporary duty assignment (TDY) from Kadena Air Force Base, Okinawa, to Da Nang, South Vietnam, along with Maj. Bill Hosmer, Lieut. Jim Hostetter, and Capt. Paul Craw from the 12th Tactical Fighter Squadron. Lieut. Col. Grant Smith from 18th Tactical Fighter Wing Operations was designated the flight leader. The purpose of the deployment was to move F-105 fighter bombers to the combat area to demonstrate a show of force.

Seven F-105s were supposed to be ready for combat duty and capable of being deployed from Kadena Air Base. I preflighted the airplane I was assigned to and found it did not pass inspection, so I was assigned to another aircraft. By the time I had preflighted this aircraft, one of the other pilots had to abort due to mechanical problems on his aircraft. That left us with a flight of five going to Da Nang.

We were scheduled to refuel north of the Philippines and managed to rendezvous with the KC-135 tanker. The flight leader succeeded in his hookup to the fuel delivery boom on the tanker, but he soon had to disconnect because he didn't have enough speed to keep up with the tanker. After another attempt, someone suggested he develop the speed needed to refuel by using his afterburner to access and maintain contact with the refueling boom of the tanker. The proper technique is to light the afterburner at midrange of the afterburner throttle position and use speed brakes to maintain a stable speed, and then use the throttle as necessary to get into position for the refueling.

Even though the lieutenant colonel was an apparently capable pilot (he was an ace in Korea), he did not know the proper technique for hooking up to the boom using an afterburner. He again hooked up to the boom, and this time when he started falling back, he went into afterburner. The acceleration caused him to pull back slightly on the stick, and when the nose of the aircraft came up slightly, his automatic response was to push forward on the stick. The nose of the aircraft dropped sharply causing the tip of the boom to break off on the receptacle of the

F-105. Fuel started pouring out of the boom while the boom operator was madly grabbing switches to shut off the fuel pump. That ended the refueling mission, and we were forced to go to Plan B and land at Clark Air Force Base in the Philippines to refuel.

Since there were no support personnel at Clark Air Force Base for the F-105, it was agreed we would all do a no drag-chute landing (drag parachutes are normally deployed after landing to slow the aircraft). Clark Air Force Base had a 13,000-foot runway, which should have been adequate without the parachute. We landed successfully. Only after we had shut down our engines did I learn that the lieutenant colonel had not only used his chute after landing, but had also burned up his tires and brakes while decelerating to a stop. No one else even had hot brakes. Capt. Paul Craw decided to stay with the lieutenant colonel while they waited for a C-130 to be dispatched from Kadena, Okinawa, with F-105 mechanics, a spare chute, new tires, and new brakes. Meanwhile, the rest of us refueled and continued on to Da Nang. I landed on Maj. Bill Hosmer's wing, and Lieut. Jim Hostetter came in number three behind us. Thus, the show of force by the United States Air Force in the Vietnam War in November 1964, consisted of three F-105s. Obviously, we did not make a great impact on public opinion!

In early 1965, the 12th and 67th Tactical Fighter Squadrons were deployed again to Da Nang, but this time as an integral part of the war effort. While operating out of Da Nang, we were assigned to bomb a road in Laos, and Maj. Paul Cleland, the assistant operations officer, asked me to prepare the flight plan. Since that area of Laos has multiple ridges and valleys that are difficult to distinguish from the air, I proposed to have the flights go to Nakhon Phanom, (code name "Naked Fanny" or NKP) on the Thailand-Laotian border, and then track outbound about forty-five miles to the target area. My plan was rejected, and there was no time to prepare another plan before takeoff. Major Cleland decided to rely on the F-105s' Doppler navigational system, and two flights of four were soon airborne to the target area.

When we arrived at the designated location, there was not enough topographical difference to any of the valleys or ridges to determine the exact location of the target. After circling for a while, the lead pilot was able to contact a photo reconnaissance pilot who was familiar enough with the target area to lead us to it. Due to heavy cloud cover, instead of rolling in at about fifteen thousand feet and having a 45-degree dive angle, we had to roll in between eight and nine thousand feet, resulting in a 25- to 30-degree dive angle. As a result, I ended up rolling in at about 300 knots and went into afterburner to build back to our normal 450-knot bomb release speed.

A second problem soon became apparent. We arrived on the target at the same time as some B-66s who were bombing the same area. As I was coming down my dive-bomb run, trying to get the pipper (bomb sight) established on the target, I noticed a B-66 coming across my path from the right at about my same altitude. Then I saw a second B-66. Needless to say, I was distracted because I wanted to look for a third one rather than track the target. I was able to avoid the B-66s and deliver the bomb load before I started my pullout from the target area. Because the target road was located up the mountainside above the valley floor, I found myself below the ridge peaks and aiming at the mountainside. During my pullout I was at about four Gs (four times the pull of normal gravity). At that point, I was doing about 500 knots, and I certainly didn't need more speed and afterburner to propel me toward that mountainside.

As I pulled out of burner, the loss of thrust and deceleration caused my whole body to move slightly forward. The stick moved forward slightly and the nose dropped. I didn't need that either. As the mountainside drew nearer, I came back sharply on the stick, so much so that I felt the F-105 going into a momentary stall at 500 knots. The G-meter registered nearly eight Gs. The maneuver caused the bomb rack, rocket pylons, and wing tanks to be thrown off the aircraft. Some of that equipment came forward, up over the wing, and tore off the leading edge devices of the wings. By the time I rejoined Major Bowersox and the rest of the flight, I had a very different looking airplane than the rest. Before landing I did a control check and found no problems. I landed without further incident. The damage to my aircraft was written off as battle damage, and thankfully, I received no reprimand.

Deployment South—Part One

by
John Morrissey, First Lieutenant
India Flight, 12th Tactical Fighter Squadron

I arrived at Kadena Air Force Base (AFB), Okinawa, in October 1963, and spent my first year with the 12th TAC Fighter Squadron (TFS) flying practice bombing missions in the F-105 fighter-bomber at target ranges on various islands surrounding Okinawa. The F-105 squadrons were also a frontline, 24-hour-a-day/365 day-per-year, nuclear weapons delivery alert force. I, along with all the 18th TAC Fighter Wing (TFW) F-105 pilots, took a ten-day turn every month on the alert-pad (the designated area for ready-alert planes and pilots capable of launch-

John Morrissey going on "the Pad", 1964

ing a retaliatory nuclear attack). It was an unthinkable scenario, but there we were on five-minute alert, with a target folder, map, pistol, radioactive dosimeter, and a sworn duty to deliver our weapon on target.

The 18th TFW had 18 of these aircraft on-line at all times, each with a 1.1 megaton nuclear weapon tucked safely inside. The only time we would launch would be after the Intercontinental Ballistic Missiles (ICBMs)—ours or theirs—were already in the air. There was an aluminized cloth shield in the cockpit that would slide forward to protect the cockpit from reflected radiation after the Mk 28 or Mk 61 detonated. After the weapon was released, the pilot would make a heads down exit dash from the area at greater than 1,100 feet per second. I don't know anyone who ever went to the pad and cocked one of those nuclear killing machines who was ever young again. I know I wasn't.

In December 1964, I was sent on temporary duty assignment (TDY) to Da Nang, South Vietnam, with a flight of four F-105s. Charlie Copin, Gene Frank, one other person whose name I have forgotten, and I made up the flight. Our mission was to fly escort for electronic intelligence gathering EC-130 flights between North Vietnam's Haiphong Harbor and Hainan Island. Every mission has a symbol indicating whether it is operational, training, combat support, or combat, but our missions

F-105 "on nuclear alert"

in flying escort for the intelligence EC-130s did not exist as far as the outside world was concerned. Therefore, we were not allowed to log these as combat missions. We were there a month and did not see any MiGs.

We flew back to Kadena AFB, and shortly thereafter the 18th TFW had an Operational Readiness Inspection (ORI). During this ORI in January 1965, the 12th TFS received orders to deploy to Da Nang, South Vietnam. Those of us who were on the alert pad were summoned, along with the rest of the squadron, and advised to go home and pack a bag; we were leaving the next morning. We knew we were going to join the war in Southeast Asia, but we did not know what our mission would be. We launched twenty-four F-105 aircraft and headed out to rendezvous with our tankers to refuel and proceed on to Da Nang. We did have cluster bomb units (CBUs) on board and 1,032 rounds of 20mm cannon ammunition in the guns. Our CBUs were on the outboard wing pods and we had two, 450-gallon gas tanks on the inboard stations of our wings. We also had multiple ejector racks underneath the fuselage that were empty, so we would be ready to load and arm bombs upon our arrival. When I stopped to think about how my airplane was configured, it became blatantly apparent that this was not a boondoggle.

When I hooked up with the tanker to take on fuel, I made an easy contact and started refueling. Unfortunately, the fuel was not going into the gas tanks; it was coming into my cockpit. I was drenched with JP-4 jet fuel. I informed Col. Bob Fair who was leading, and upon his orders, I was sent to Clark Field in the Philippines to get fuel, get cleaned up, and then meet the squadron in Da Nang later that day.

Of course, we did not go anywhere single ship, so he sent my assistant flight commander, Gene Frank, to accompany me. After we landed at Clark, I went into base Ops (operations), took off my flight suit and showered, put it back on, jumped back in the shower, and washed again. The flight suit was still sopping wet when I got back in the plane, but I felt pretty confident that with the air-conditioning system, I would quickly "cool-dry".

After flying the long flight to Da Nang, we found the weather was at "minimums" (half-mile visibility) for landing and we had no opportunity for in-flight refueling or an alternate landing site. The only other available airfield was Saigon, 400 miles to the south, and we would never have enough fuel to get there if we missed our approach into Da Nang. We decided, that despite the weather, we were going to Da Nang. We did not want to be late and run the risk of not catching up with our squadron, or, even worse, get orders to be sent back home. Gene Frank was leading, and I, a young lieutenant, was flying on his wing. When we got to Da Nang, Gene reported that his altitude and heading indicators were not functioning and that he would have to land on my wing. We made a GCA (ground control approach) and landed satisfactorily, breaking out of the overcast a little below minimums. As we broke out of the clouds at low level, there was the runway. We landed in formation, taxied in, and shut down, happy to be on the ground.

After several days of inactivity and some road and bridge attacks in Laos, we received orders to return to Kadena. However, on February 7, 1965, the night prior to our departure, an overwhelming enemy attack on a U.S. Army base at Pleiku in the central highlands increased the intensity of the war and the U.S. commitment. The attack cost the Americans seven dead and more than one hundred wounded. A few days later, on February 10, 1965, the enemy blew up a barracks near Qui Nhon. Twenty-three Americans died and 22 were wounded. All of a sudden, this was not just a civil war between North and South—it had become an American war.

All of our F-105 aircraft were configured with external fuel tanks and no bombs for the flight back to Okinawa. I was the duty officer on the night of February 7, when the call came in from headquarters in Saigon to download those tanks and upload the bomb racks again. The message was sent in "the clear" without codes and with no apologies. We, the USAF, were going to attack targets in North Vietnam for the first time. The mission was to hit Vinh, North Vietnam, on February 8, 1965.

The weather at Da Nang the next morning was bad, with 1,000-foot overcast, and in the target area was no better. But somehow, in the early stages of the war, the decision was made to go. There was a squadron of F-100s on temporary duty assignment (TDY) from England Air Force Base in Alexandria, Louisiana, with whom we shared the ramp. The F-100s went out and lined up their whole squadron on the runway and launched. Then our squadron of F-105s lined up on the runway and prepared to launch. Just then, a Navy jet aircraft coming back from an attack on Vinh approached, low on fuel, and unable to get back to his carrier. Our squadron was lined up to take off to the south, so the Navy plane made an approach to the north and went around. Then he made another approach to the north and went around again, and on the third approach he landed, with his gear up on the only runway available, heading directly toward our airplanes. He had two Mark 81 two-hundred-fifty-pound bombs on board and one Zuni rocket. He slid down the runway toward us, trailing fire, and the Mark 81s blew up under his airplane "low order" (incomplete explosion), but it was enough to rock him and put a hole in the runway. Because we soon would have to recover the twenty-four F-100s, crews went out with a crane and removed his aircraft, cleaned up the runway, and filled the hole. Well, of course, our F-105 guys had to taxi back in and shut down. We were all disappointed. The F-100s returned, but had not been able to expend their ordnance because the weather was too low in the target area. All in all, the USAF's first day in the war over North Vietnam was quite a bust.

Deployment South—Part Two
Bug-Out to Korat

by
John Morrissey, First Lieutenant
India Flight, 12th Tactical Fighter Squadron

There was a F-102 interceptor squadron on the base at Da Nang that was supposed to protect the field and keep it safe from aerial attack by Russian MiG airplanes flown by the North Vietnamese. The 102s were down at the south end of the field and they had a small horse for a mascot. I got the great idea one night at the DOOM club (Da Nang Officers Open Mess) that I would go down and "borrow" the horse and ride it up to the bar at the Officers Club, and order a drink.

That very night, while I was sitting on the horse having a drink at the bar, the base commander walked in rather briskly and said, "You 105 jocks—saddle-up and get the hell out of here; the Viet Cong are reported to be planning an attack on Da Nang Air Force Base. I have no ground troops to protect the base—or your airplanes. I don't want the responsibility of losing a whole squadron of planes and pilots from mortar or ground attack. Arrangements have been made for you to go to Korat, Thailand. Get your gear and your planes and get moving."

Three hours later, we were rolling down the runway heading west to Thailand. The night was extremely dark. I think there were only four light bulbs in all of Indochina, and they were all turned off that night. It was just pitch black. Fighter pilots in those days did not fly much at night, and when they did, they went up when there was moonlight. When we arrived at Korat, there were so few runway lights they had to put some flare pots out to help us land.

For the next eight years, combat missions were flown over North Vietnam, Laos, and the Ho Chi Minh Trail from bases in Thailand by the United States Air Force and from carrier-based naval aircraft at Yankee Station in the Gulf of Tonkin. As far as the rest of the world knew, the Thailand based missions were all being flown out of Da Nang, South Vietnam. In addition to our squadrons from the 18th Tactical Fighter Wing, Kadena Air Force Base, Okinawa, F-105 squadrons from

McConnell Air Force Base, Kansas, were also flying missions out of both Korat and Takhli, Thailand. The news media was not allowed access to the Thailand bases or to our pilots.

President Lyndon Johnson ordered the landing of two United States Marine battalions at Da Nang, South Vietnam, on March 8, 1965, to protect the air base. It was the first major commitment of U.S. ground troops to the Vietnam War.

Lowell Peterson

First Raid North

by
Bill Hosmer, Major
Flight Commander, Lima Flight, 12th Tactical Fighter Squadron

On March 2, 1965, the 2nd Air Division headquarters in Saigon ordered the first strike into North Vietnam by the United States Air Force. The target was Xom Bang, located in the southern reaches of North Vietnam, later to be designated as the Pack One area. Our target was a munitions storage complex.

The strike plan, detailed in specifics, called for F-100 aircraft from Da Nang, South Vietnam, and multiple F-105s from the 12th and 67th Tactical Fighter Squadrons (TFS) of the 18th Tactical Fighter Wing (TFW) from Korat, Thailand, to attack the target. The strike leader of the force of F-105s was Col. Robinson "Robbie" Risner, and I was leading the second flight of four aircraft. The F-100s were in the target area before we arrived, and we attacked the target after they departed. During the course of the mission, it was obvious to me that there were too many planes concentrated in too small an airspace with unrealistic assigned times on the target.

There were aircraft shot down that day. Most were rescued, but one F-100 pilot, Hayden Lockhart, was captured and spent eight years as a prisoner of war of the North Vietnamese. Boris Baird, flying with Colonel Risner's flight, was shot down and was rescued. Baird and Lockhart were quite close together after ejection, but they landed with a ridge separating them. It became a "heartbreak ridge" that separated the lucky from the unlucky. Ken Spagnola and George Pannus were shot down in the same general area and recovered. An F-100 was also shot down at Vinh that same day but I am not sure of the fate of the pilot.

After the mission, Colonel Risner obtained approval to visit 2nd Air Division Headquarters to suggest some changes and make recommendations regarding subsequent mission orders. Col. "Robbie" Risner, Col. Grant Smith (Assistant Director of Operations, 18th TFW), and I flew to Saigon on March 3, 1965, to meet with General Moore and his staff at 2nd Air Division. We presented our concerns about the difficulty in executing strikes with dense concentrations of aircraft. We were very specific in describing the parameters, striving for less force, with fewer airplanes, on any given target, at any given time. Evidently, someone heard us because the next strike into North Vietnam directed at another munitions storage area in the same pack one area used fewer aircraft and more manageable times on target. Unfortunately, in spite of our temporary reprieve, the flawed reasoning behind the March 2 orders—large numbers of airplanes, with tight times on target, dropping a lot of bombs and punching a lot of holes in the ground—continued to be the overriding directive.

Because target selection and force deployment were under such tight control from the White House and the Defense Department, photographic evidence had to be provided that the missions were efficacious. This flawed strategy and misplaced emphasis of purpose became much more apparent to me later in 1965 when we began to strike the surface-to-air missile (SAM) sites. When I reiterated my concerns, again recommending fewer numbers of aircraft for any given strike, Brig. Gen. George Simler assured me he would try to represent my thoughts fairly to 2nd Air Division (and through them, to the Defense Department and Secretary McNamara). "But," he said, "they like to see a lot of bomb craters in post-strike photos."

Robbie

by
Frank Tullo, First Lieutenant
Lima Flight, 12th Tactical Fighter Squadron

Col. Robinson "Robbie" Risner, the commander of our sister squadron, the 67th TAC Fighter Squadron (TFS) was fearless; no braver than anybody else, but totally fearless. He would make numerous passes at a target if necessary, with little concern for his own safety. I was in his flight the day of his first shoot down. I was flying number four in our flight and "Hoz" (Bill Hosmer) was number three. The story of what happened on that day was recorded in an interview with Colonel Risner by *Time* magazine in the April 23, 1965, issue. Robbie told it this way:

> *The target that day was a radar station in North Vietnam. I was jinking around (changing altitude and direction continuously) when I got hit by ground fire. They got me four feet behind the cockpit, in the engine. I had to make a 180-degree turn to get out over the sea. When I got to the coastline, I figured I was safe. But in the water was an enemy gunboat, so I had to keep on going. Suddenly, the plane flipped over and I was flying upside down. I flew about three-fourths of a mile that way. Then I reached down and pulled the seat handles, which flipped off the canopy. Then I groped until I found the ejection handles. I was still pulling them when the butt-snapper (that's a canvas that snaps taut and flips you clear) under the seat propelled me into the air. Three swift jolts and I was floating down in my parachute. I inflated my Mae West and released my rubber dinghy about twenty-five feet from the water. Seconds after touching down, I was in the dinghy. Fifty seconds later, I had ripped open my survival kit, set the squak-radio beam going, activated my 11-hp radio, and called Thunderbird Two. The first thing I asked him was whether he had sunk that gunboat. He said he had cut it in two with his 20mm cannon. Then I asked if Dumbo (a rescue seaplane) was coming, and he said right away. The Dumbo landed a few minutes later and picked me up. Fear is*

a luxury one can't afford. I believe in God. I'm already at peace with myself. If death comes, I only hope it comes quickly and that I won't be sorry.

Risner bailed out over the Gulf and waited for Air Sea Rescue to take him out of the water from his one-man life raft. The rest of us were flying cover over him, as enemy boats were coming out from shore to capture him. We had our 20mm cannons and we were cutting those boats in half, but more of them just kept on coming. Robbie later told me that as the Dumbo plane was picking him out of the water, the boats were so close that a piece of the boat we destroyed flew right over the top of his head. After Risner's rescue, "Hoz" and I headed back to base. I was a young lieutenant at the time, and I had just experienced my first thrilling taste of combat. As I flew along, the adrenaline totally wrung out of me, I noted that my flight suit was totally soaked with sweat. I took off my oxygen mask and tried to light a cigarette. I wiped my mouth and it was all covered with foam. I thought, "Jesus Christ, I'm foaming at the mouth!" I was that scared!

The Dragon's Jaw

by
John Morrissey, First Lieutenant
India Flight, 12th Tactical Fighter Squadron

The Than Hoa (Than-Wa) railroad and highway bridge, spanning the Song Ma River, is located three miles north of the city of Than Hoa, the capitol of Annam Province, North Vietnam. The bridge, completed in 1964, was 540 feet long, 56 feet wide, and 50 feet above the river. The Vietnamese called it Ham Rong (Dragon's Jaw). A narrow-gauge railroad track ran down the center, flanked on

Than Hoa Bridge under attack by F-105s - July 24, 1965. Photo courtesy of Captain James R. Hostetter

either side by 22-foot wide reinforced concrete highways. This giant would prove to be one of the single most challenging targets for American air power during the Vietnam War.

In March 1965, the decision to interdict the North Vietnamese rail system south of the 20th Parallel led to the April 3, 1965, strike against the bridge. Lt. Col. Robinson Risner was designated the mission coordinator. He assembled a force of 79 aircraft—46 F-105s, 21 F-100s, 2 RF-101 reconnaissance aircraft, and 10 KC-135 tankers. Sixteen of the Thuds (F-105s) were loaded with pairs of bullpup missiles, and each of the remaining 30 carried eight 750-pound general-purpose bombs. Flights of four F-105s from Korat and Takhli, Thailand, would be air-refueled over the Mekong River before proceeding across Laos to an initial point (IP) three minutes south of the bridge. After weapon release, the aircraft were to continue east and rejoin over the Gulf of Tonkin where a Navy destroyer would be available to recover anyone who had to eject due to battle damage.

Shortly after noon on April 3, aircraft of Rolling Thunder mission 9-Alpha climbed into the skies of Southeast Asia on their journey to the Than Hoa Bridge. Colonel Risner led the way, and soon missiles and bombs were exploding on the target. Since only one bullpup missile could be fired at a time, each plane carrying this weapon had to make two firing passes. On his second pass, Risner's aircraft was hit by antiaircraft fire just as the bullpup hit the bridge. Fighting a serious fuel leak and a smoke-filled cockpit, Colonel Risner was able to fly his crippled aircraft to safety at Da Nang, South Vietnam.

Destroyed Than Hoa Bridge

When the smoke cleared, observer aircraft found that the bridge still spanned the river. Thirty-two bullpups and 10-dozen 750-pound bombs had been aimed at the bridge, scoring numerous hits, but no sign of significant damage to the structure had occurred. A restrike was ordered for the next day.

On this day, Capt. Carlyle "Smitty" Harris oriented himself on a 300-degree heading for his bomb run on the bridge, reporting that his

New Than Hoa Bridge
Photo courtesy of John Morrissey

bombs had impacted on target. Unfortunately, it was noted that Smitty's aircraft was on fire as soon as he left the target. His fellow flight members had him in sight until the fire died out, but observed no parachute. His plane had been hit by a missile fired from a North Vietnamese MiG jet fighter, the first such attack on an American aircraft. It was found out later that Smitty had bailed out successfully, was captured, and made a prisoner of war. Although over 300 bombs scored hits on this second strike, the bridge still stood.

In these first two days of attacks, six aircraft were lost, three pilots were missing-in-action, and three were captured. From April to September 1965, 19 more pilots were shot down in the general vicinity of the Dragon, including, on September 16, Col. Robbie Risner. He was held as a POW for the next 7$1/2$ years, spending 4$1/2$ years in solitary confinement.

Further innovative attempts to destroy the bridge were launched in the ensuing years with 3,000 pound bombs and updated "Walleye" missiles, but all attempts failed to knock out the bridge. A mission on July 28, 1965, was led by Lt. Col. Charles W. Reed, 12th TFS commander. The call-sign was Teak. Teak-2 was Capt. Wesley G. Carey; Teak-3 was Maj. William J. Hosmer; Teak-4 was Capt. James R. Hostetter; and, Teak-5 carrying camera pods was Capt. Samuel E. Waters, Jr. (later shot down and killed-in-action). Before the war ended, 104 American pilots were shot down over a 75-square-mile area around the Dragon's Jaw.

Years of attack on the Than Hoa Bridge involving some 800 sorties and the loss of multiple airplanes, failed to destroy the target. Precision weapons—laser-guided bombs first proved successful in 1972—were eventually utilized and the bridge fell.

Voluntary Grounding

by
Lowell Peterson, Captain
Flight Surgeon, 12th Tactical Fighter Squadron

I had just arrived at the 6332nd USAF Dispensary at 0730 on a Monday morning in early 1965, still shaking the cobwebs out of my head from a weekend of parties that were so prevalent at Kadena Air Force Base. I was contemplating what drudgery lay ahead in my 24-hour shift as the Medical Officer of the Day (MOD) when a corpsman met me at the door, saying, "Doc, there's a pilot waiting outside your office who insists on talking to you."

What was this all about, I wondered. Probably a new pilot wanting to get his flight physical done without an appointment, or possibly a pilot who took a skoshi-cab into Koza or Futenma and now was nervously going to request a shot of penicillin.

I went out into the hallway and saw a man pacing back and forth. He was tall, athletic, and handsome. As I approached, he stopped pacing and almost came to attention. I saw his captain's bars on his collar and his name tag above the right shirt pocket read "Williamson".

"Captain Williamson, are you waiting to see me? I'm Captain Peterson, a flight surgeon, but just call me Doc." I tried to keep my tone of voice relaxed, hoping that I could diffuse some of the anxiety I sensed.

He put out his hand to shake mine and said, "Just call me Don or Donnie. I'm new to the 12th Squadron, and I understand that you're our flight surgeon. I'd like a few moments of your time, if that's okay."

I acknowledged that I was attached to the 12th, but at times was required to work in the general medical clinic seeing military personnel and their dependents. After I invited him to have a seat in my office, Donnie quickly got to the point.

"Doc, can I be frank with you?" he asked.

"Of course, Don, what's on your mind?" I asked.

"Doc, I want you to ground me," he answered.

I could not believe what I was hearing. Pilots rarely came to the flight surgeon's office for medical problems, and when they did, they just wanted a quick fix and would beg not to be grounded. Groundings went on their records and they did not want that. After I got over my shock, I asked, "Donnie, why do you want to be grounded?"

He was very candid. He said, "Doc, the personnel people are screwing me over and I can't keep my mind on my flying. They've lost my housing requisitions, they can't find my wife's embarkation orders to leave the U.S., and now they say that because I haven't been on Okinawa for six weeks, I have to start all over again, redoing all the paperwork. I can't fly with all this crap going on. That F-105 out there can kill me if I don't tend to business, and I don't intend for that to happen."

I was stunned that he wanted to be grounded for administrative reasons, but as I assessed the situation, I recognized that he was absolutely correct, and I admired his honesty. "Captain Williamson, as of now, you're grounded," I told him. "I'll call your squadron commander and tell him you've got the shits, and unless he wants you messing up the inside of a shiny new F-105, he had better go along with this." No commanding officer in his right mind was going to contradict a doctor's judgment in matters like this. Then I told Donnie that after he had everything under control and his wife was on her way, he should come back to me and I would declare that he had recovered.

As we moved toward the door, I shook his hand and told him that it was a pleasure to know him. Before he left, I asked him what flight he was assigned to.

"I'm in Lima Flight. Come on down and fly with me someday."

That opportunity never came, but if it had, I would have done so with the utmost confidence.

Boo-Boo and Susie

by
Lowell Peterson, Captain
Flight Surgeon, 12th Tactical Fighter Squadron

After an interminable ten-hour flight from Kadena Air Force Base, Okinawa, our C-54 landed at Korat, Thailand, on June 16, 1965. I had been to Korat during Operation Air Boon Choo a year previously, so the trip and the destination were familiar, but the mood this time was different. I sensed a strange mixture of ambivalent feelings in the F-105 pilots of the 12th Tactical Fighter Squadron (TFS) who were also aboard. The atmosphere was quiet and reserved—atypical of fighter pilots. Some were engrossed in reading, and others played low-stakes poker or gin rummy. Trying to start a conversation with them had left me with an empty feeling, so I also leaned back, periodically dozed, or read magazines as my mind joined theirs in contemplating what lay ahead.

The 12th TFS was replacing the 44th TFS, which had been flying combat missions the past two months over North Vietnam, Laos, and the Ho Chi Minh Trail. Now it was our turn. We were at war and we all knew it.

As we approached the base, the near melancholy suddenly changed to anxious anticipation and gung-ho bravado. "Let us at those sons-of-bitches," I heard. "We'll kick their ass and make those commies know who's going to win this damn thing!" I got caught up in the spirit and found it a relief from the unnerving quiet of the trip. A bunch of "shit-hot" fighter pilots had just arrived to assume the command on the front lines of the air war and they meant to get the job done. I could sense the pent-up energy of the pilots as the C-54 shut down its engines, the door opened, and the stairway was placed against the side of the fuselage. As the 12th squadron pilots exited the plane, a huge cheer went up from the guys of the 44th who

Boo-Boo

43

had assembled to meet us.

After greeting each other with hugs, handshakes, and pats on the back, our group started quizzing the veteran pilots—"What's it been like up north? How bad's the flak? Missiles? MiGs?" Finally, our guys either got the information they desired or concluded that there was no way to adequately assess the situation except firsthand, so they moved on to less intense subjects.

A popular topic with the 44th guys was about two barmaids at the Officers Club—Boo-Boo and Susie. One said, "Susie's cute as hell and Boo-Boo is downright beautiful."

"They will knock your socks off," the other said.

I was told that they were Thai girls who spoke English, tended bar like they had been trained at the Waldorf, and dressed like American girls. All the men agreed, they were really "shit-hot!"

Unfortunately, before we could adjourn to the Officers Club to meet Boo-Boo and Susie, we all had to go for an initial formal briefing from Lieut. Col. Robert "Bob" Fair, a former 12th squadron commander. He was the Operations Officer and ran flight operations for the deployed squadrons. He had blond curly hair, rosy cheeks, a slight paunch, and a bit of a knock-kneed stance. He told us what the air war at that point in time was really like. I recall his briefing very well. It went like this:

> Gentlemen, welcome to Korat. Tomorrow morning, you will begin flying combat sorties over North Vietnam, Laos, and the Ho Chi Minh Trail. You will have no period of grace. You will fly tomorrow as if you had been here for months. There is no break-in-period to get used to things. The missions assigned to us come from the command system in Saigon, as directed by the Defense Department in Washington, DC. We follow orders and we assign the missions accordingly. Just remember one thing—and this is not official; this is me talking confidentially to each of you—there is not, I repeat NOT a single target that we are assigned to attack that is worth going below 6,000 feet to hit. Below that, you are in the range of small arms fire and light artillery. We have to deal with flak and the 50mm and 88mm antiaircraft artillery, but we do not have to get blown out of the sky by some yak-driving farmer with a popgun. Protect yourself, protect your wingmen, look out for each other, and come back safe and in one piece.

> *Your flight assignments will be posted here on the bulletin board. This is a secure area. Keep it that way! Weather evaluation flights begin briefing at 0500 and leave at 0600. The other flights brief at 0900, with sorties starting at 1000 hours. Intelligence and weather briefings will be in this room and then you will break out and go to the base flight area for your individual flight briefings. I want to remind you to leave all personal belongings in your locker or at your hooch. Do not have billfolds, pictures, letters, or memorabilia on your person when you fly. If you are shot down, they can be used against you by the enemy. If you want to carry something other than your dog tags, make it a rabbit's foot.*

The briefing broke up with small talk and more questions that had no answers. Our guys were now on their own.

We all adjourned to the "O" Club at Camp Nasty to find relaxation at the throne of Boo-Boo and Susie. The club was an L-shaped hooch with a few tables and a long bar with lots of stools. I wasn't disappointed. Boo-Boo and Susie were everything I had been told to expect. They greeted us with wide-toothy smiles and a, "Hi, flyboys." The 44th and 12th squadrons, sat together as brothers, each knowing the agony of the other. The 44th had already lost pilots to captivity and the 12th was soon to fly the same dangerous path. The alcohol poured by Boo-Boo and Susie soothed wounds that had occurred and those that were yet to come.

The noise grew louder and the conversation more raucous as the evening wore on, but the unspoken question—"Is this my final night on earth?"—was sublimated below the surface of the conscious mind. As the party wore down and the reality set in that it was time to prepare for our mission, the mood again became somber.

Before the bar closed for the night, Boo-Boo and Susie bought a drink for everybody, and Boo-Boo announced in her high-pitched voice, "Don't worry flyboys; you, 44th, will be back. I wait for you! You, 12th, I love you, too. We make big party for next two months. You fly airplanes; I mix drinks. We have fun. Don't worry, you all go home to Mama!"

They were simple words, even silly, I suppose, but they came across like a peptalk—one that was as good as any college coach could deliver, and more profound than I can logically explain. The next day, the 12th saddled-up to fly in the F-105s and the 44th went home in the C-54, both cushioned on the air of the words of a barmaid named Boo-Boo at Camp Nasty.

III
THE TURNING POINT
JULY 24 - 27, 1965

The air war over the North and in Laos and Cambodia was waged in fits and starts, in secret and in the open, covered by lies and subterfuge, manipulated more by opinion polls than by military exigencies ... even the State Department was allowed to veto air strikes. President Johnson stayed up late calling the plays while generals were sidelined.

Melvin R. Laird
2005

TEMPORARY DUTY ORDER—MILITARY

(If more space is required, continue on reverse, identifying items by number)

DATE	10 June 1965

TO: Hq 18 Tac Ftr Wg (18AS)	FROM: Hq 18 Tac Ftr Wg (18DCOT)	1. INDIVIDUAL(S) WP ON TDY AS SHOWN IN ITEMS 5 THROUGH 21.

2. TYPED NAME, GRADE AND TITLE OF ORDERS ISSUING OFFICIAL JOHN C NEILL, Lt Colonel, USAF Asst Deputy Commander for Operations	3. SIGNATURE *John C Neill*	4. PHONE NO. 41203

5. GRADE	6. NAME *(Last, first, middle initial, AFSN)*		7. ORGANIZATION	8. SECURITY CLEARANCE
LT COL	REED CHARLES W, 12722A	(J20)	12 Tac Ftr Sq	TOP SECRET
MAJOR	CLELAND PAUL S JR, 44364A	(J20)	12 Tac Ftr Sq	TOP SECRET
MAJOR	BOWERSOX RALPH H, 30831A	(J20)	12 Tac Ftr Sq	TOP SECRET
	(See reverse side)			

9. EFFECTIVE ON OR ABOUT 18 June 65	10. APPROXIMATE NO. OF DAYS *(Include travel time)* 60	11. 0 DDALV

12. PURPOSE OF TDY In support of PACAF OPORD 131-65	13. ITINERARY FROM: Kadena AB APO 96239 TO: Korat AB Thailand RETURN TO: Kadena AB APO 96239	☒ VARIATIONS AUTHORIZED

Reverse side items 5, 6, 7 and 8 continued:

MAJOR	HOSMER WILLIAM J, 25123A	(J20)	12 Tac Ftr Sq	TOP SECRET
CAPT	COPIN CHARLES, A03026341	(J20)	12 Tac Ftr Sq	TOP SECRET
CAPT	CROMACK DANA B, 47148A	(J20)	12 Tac Ftr Sq	TOP SECRET
CAPT	MATTHEWS HARRISON W, 28842A	(J20)	12 Tac Ftr Sq	TOP SECRET
CAPT	WILLIAMSON DON I, 46788A	(J20)	12 Tac Ftr Sq	TOP SECRET
CAPT	FRANK VERNON E, A03038231	(J20)	12 Tac Ftr Sq	TOP SECRET
CAPT	PURCELL ROBERT B, 53786A	(J20)	12 Tac Ftr Sq	TOP SECRET
CAPT	SMITH DONALD F, 53872A	(J20)	12 Tac Ftr Sq	TOP SECRET
CAPT	STREET JAMES F, A02246276	(J17)	18 Tac Ftr Wg	TOP SECRET
CAPT	MOSS RAYMOND V, A03058315	(J20)	12 Tac Ftr Sq	TOP SECRET
CAPT	JONES JOHN C, A03064899	(J20)	12 Tac Ftr Sq	TOP SECRET
CAPT	BOATMAN THOMAS E, A03038565	(J20)	12 Tac Ftr Sq	TOP SECRET
CAPT	BUSBEE JOHN H, A03080241	(J20)	12 Tac Ftr Sq	TOP SECRET
CAPT	BOGERT GEORGE A, 67267A	(J20)	12 Tac Ftr Sq	TOP SECRET
A2C	BELTON HERBERT L JR, AF13789710	(J20)	12 Tac Ftr Sq	TOP SECRET
CAPT	YEOKUM CHARLES M, 68382A	(J20)	12 Tac Ftr Sq	TOP SECRET
CAPT	CAREY WESLEY G JR, 68669A	(J20)	12 Tac Ftr Sq	TOP SECRET
CAPT	CRANE ROBERT M, A03103370	(J20)	12 Tac Ftr Sq	TOP SECRET
CAPT	WATERS SAMUEL E JR, 59427A	(J20)	12 Tac Ftr Sq	TOP SECRET
1ST LT	HOSTETTER JAMES R, A03117117	(J20)	12 Tac Ftr Sq	TOP SECRET
1ST LT	TULLO FRANK J, 74077A	(J20)	12 Tac Ftr Sq	TOP SECRET
1ST LT	MORRISSEY JOHN C, 74926A	(J20)	12 Tac Ftr Sq	TOP SECRET
1ST LT	O'HARA CHARLES P, A03137216		824 Cmbt Spt Gp	TOP SECRET
1ST LT	LARGE CHARLES C, A03108688	(J20)	12 Tac Ftr Sq	TOP SECRET
TSGT	COVILLE GERALD K, AF16268632	(J20)	12 Tac Ftr Sq	TOP SECRET
CAPT	PETERSON LOWELL F, A03126846		Det 4 1 Med Svc Wg	TOP SECRET

Item 22 continued:

Budget Accounting Classfication Section (funding citation). See AFM 170-7.
Travel within Bangkok or Don Muang Thailand. Transportation is available
between Don Muang AB and Bangkok between the hours of 0615 and 2200 hrs daily.
Specific evidence that mission requirements necessitated use of other than
existing transportation. Personnel will report to the senior AF commander and
inform him of date of arrival, destination and purpose of TDY. The concurrence
of the commanders concerned has been obtained.

Dark Days of July

by
Lowell Peterson, Captain
Flight Surgeon, 12th Tactical Fighter Squadron

This is not the end, maybe not even the beginning of
the end. But it is, perhaps, the end of the beginning.
                                        Winston Churchill
                                        1942

On June 16, 1965, I was deployed on temporary duty assignment (TDY) from Kadena Air Force Base (AFB), Okinawa, with the 12th Tactical Fighter Squadron (TFS) to Korat, Thailand. I was the flight surgeon for the squadron and I was about to get my first taste of what it was like to be in a combat zone with fighter pilots who were flying missions over North Vietnam. F-105 squadrons from McConnell AFB, Kansas, were also TDY, flying missions out of both Korat and Takhli, Thailand. As far as the rest of the world knew, these missions were all being flown out of Da Nang, South Vietnam. During our TDY, reporters from *Time* magazine came to Korat to do a story, but were quickly gone, forbidden to interview our pilots or report what they had seen because of a gag order from the Pentagon.

The number of F-105 combat sorties flown in the spring and early summer of 1965 progressively increased during operation Rolling Thunder, which had been initiated on direct order from President Johnson in February 1965. The purpose of this bombing campaign into North Vietnam was to destroy military supply depots in the north and interdict supplies from reaching communist forces in South Vietnam along the Ho Chi Minh Trail. In addition, it was hoped the bombing would force North Vietnam to negotiate a peace that would preclude the need to send more ground troops to South Vietnam.

But, the North Vietnamese raids did little to slow the flow of supplies and there was no indication of a willingness to negotiate. The F-105 pilots were coming under attack from small arms fire, antiaircraft artillery, an increasing threat from SA-2 surface-to-air missiles (SAMs), and MiG fighter planes. Antiaircraft artillery around cities, bridges, factories, fuel storage facilities, and rail yards was horrendous. Returning pilots described the black puffs of smoke from antiaircraft flak bursts as a patchwork of stepping stones in the sky. The North Vietnamese were vigorously defending their resources from attack as well as protecting major roads and bridges used for shipment of war materials.

By order of the President, the Secretary of Defense, and the Joint Chiefs of Staff, there was a restricted 30-mile no-fly zone for U.S. pilots around Hanoi and a similar buffer at the Chinese border. U.S. pilots were forced to fly past dams, factories, airfields filled with airplanes, and other tempting targets because they had been declared off-limits by the U.S. government. Any transgression of these orders would result in a court-martial. Because of the restrictions, flight routes became predictable, and as F-105 pilot Frank Tullo noted, "We continually telegraphed what we were going to do." As a result, numerous planes were shot down and many pilots became prisoners of war at Hoa Lo Prison, the "Hanoi Hilton". Some—mostly carrier-based Navy pilots—were fortunate enough to fly their disabled planes out over the Gulf of Tonkin before ejecting, which markedly increased their chance for safe recovery. Because the Air Force F-105s and F-4Cs flying out of Thailand were assigned targets far from the coast in zones to the north and west of Hanoi and along the Vietnam-Laos border and in Laos itself, their odds of recovery after a bailout were less favorable. Evasion and escape was almost impossible.

In 1965, the North Vietnamese started deploying Russian-made, fan-song radar-guided surface-to-air missiles with Russian advisors reportedly manning them. These SAMs were very mobile. They were here one day, somewhere else the next, always camouflaged, and a threat to all American aircraft. The fear of involving the U.S.S.R. in the war made the U.S. government reluctant to aggressively search out and destroy the missile sites.

Apprehension and frustration continued to rise among U.S. pilots as the threat grew greater and the countermeasures remained weak and ineffective. EB-66 electronic and countermeasure (ECM) aircraft were brought in to be airborne during missions. These aircraft did not have any effective method for electronically jamming the radars of the SAMs, but at least they could identify when the radars became active. The North Vietnamese, or their Russian advisors, often would turn on the radar guidance system just long enough to threaten the invading U.S. pilots, but not long enough to reveal their own location. The ECM surveillance planes would report when the radar was active by a radio message to the fighter pilots saying, "The bluebells are singing."

In the summer of 1965, a decision was made to pursue low-level bombing in anticipation of specifically targeting SAM sites. The idea was that it made more sense to identify a missile site by aerial intelligence, attack it at low level and high speed with appropriate weaponry from different directions, and then evacuate the area. Brig. Gen. George Simler, a former 18th TFW commander at Kadena Air Base, was on-site at Korat for a period of time in July 1965 as this low-level bombing plan was initiated. I remember seeing him resting on a bench, his flying suit sweaty in the heat, his feet up revealing cowboy boots. He was obviously deep in thought. Needless to say, no one bothered him. As a result of General Simler's recommendations to headquarters, the pilots received permission to drop down and practice low-level flying and low-level target approaches.

After all the preparation and practice, the feeling among our 12th Squadron pilots was that we finally had some input on how to execute the air war, utilizing a minimum number of airplanes with a maximum element of surprise.

However, it was not to be. On July 24, four F-4C American aircraft were attacked by SAM missiles for the first time. As a result of this action, Secretary of Defense Robert McNamara ordered operation Iron Hand, a mass-gaggle, maximum effort attack on two SAM sites with forty-eight airplanes. After all the work, planning, and preparation, the message was completely different; we had not been listened to at all! A palpable gloom settled over the base.

Don Williamson

by
Frank Tullo, First Lieutenant
Lima Flight, 12th Tactical Fighter Squadron

On July 7, 1965, I was leading a flight of four F-105s, with each plane carrying six 750-pound bombs and two canisters of 2.75 rockets. Donnie Williamson and I swapped positions every time we flew a mission together. It was my turn to lead, so he flew as number two. Flying number three was J. C. Jones; number four was Chuck Hofelich. The targets were two small bridges about a half a mile apart southwest of Vinh in North Vietnam. We decided that after refueling from the tanker, we would fly to the target at about 13,000 feet. Donnie and I would roll in on the first bridge and drop the six 750s, and numbers three and four would fly down to the next target and do the same. After our bombing runs, we would look for targets of opportunity on a road that we had been assigned in order to fire our rockets or use our cannon fire.

Flying as spare, or number five, that day was Maj. Ralph Bowersox, the squadron operations officer. He flew to the tanker with us, but, after taking on fuel he was to return to base while we were to fly to the target. However, he decided to stay in the area and listen to our radio calls.

Frank Tullo and Don Williamson July 7, 1965—
leaving on a fateful mission (frame from a Super-8 movie)

This proved to be fortunate for us.

We approached our target, and as I rolled into a 45-degree dive-bomb run on the small bridge, I saw no sign of antiaircraft flak. That was good news and rather unusual; we always saw flak. I dropped my bombs on the target, and as I started to pull out, I heard number three call out, "Lead, you're on fire!" I checked my instruments for any signs that I was hit, and seeing none, I turned to my right, and saw Donnie pulling out of the bombing run behind me. He was on fire!

J. C. and I made a couple of calls to Donnie telling him he was on fire, but we never got any response. He pulled out of the bombing run with a nose-up angle of 20 degrees, getting slower and slower. I positioned myself on his right wing, and as he climbed above five thousand feet, the canopy came off and he ejected. I saw smoke rolling out of the cockpit. I turned hard to the left in order to keep his parachute in sight and then made a fly-by of him in the chute. As I flew by, he made no attempt to look at me. He appeared to be looking straight down.

J. C. and Chuck went to altitude, making radio calls to arrange a rescue attempt. This was standard operating procedure. I stayed low with Donnie, trying to fix the position where he landed. I tried to time my next pass so that I was flying by just as he hit the ground. He landed in a field covered in grass, and there were piles of hay in the field. Small villages and clumps of trees dotted the area. I was able to come in low and observe him land and watch his chute spill out on the ground. As I passed over him, he appeared to be lying on the ground. When I pulled up from that pass, I inadvertently flew directly over the gun emplacement that had fired on us during the bombing run. I saw tracer bullets flying by and felt a thump. I looked out and saw that the tip of my right wing had taken a hit. I maneuvered around and made another pass over Donnie without flying over the flak site. I saw nothing. The chute was gone and there was no sign of Donnie. At that moment, I assumed that he had gathered up his chute and run to the nearest cover.

I made many calls on our emergency guard channel radio frequency, expecting to hear Donnie respond, but he never did. I knew he had two emergency radios, which we all carried, but I never heard anything. While over the ejection site, I neither heard nor saw anything that would have convinced me that Donnie was trying to contact me.

Because I had a limited amount of fuel, I needed to return to the tanker on the other side of the Thai border. I decided that the best way to conserve fuel was to jettison all of my stores and clean the aircraft. I did this, but almost instantly realized that by jettisoning my external fuel tanks, I had limited the time that I could stay in the ejection area after refueling. I was getting real low on fuel when two Navy A-1 Sky Raiders arrived to relieve me. J. C. and Chuck had done a good job of arranging the rescue attempt. I pointed out the area where Donnie had landed, warned them of the flak, and headed west to the tanker.

I was pleasantly surprised to find number five, Major Bowersox, at the tanker. As I hooked up to the tanker and was taking on fuel, he looked my plane over and told me that the only damage to my bird was the right wing tip. He topped off his fuel from the tanker and we returned to the shoot-down site in North Vietnam as a flight of two. We never joined up with numbers three and four of the flight, but we heard them in the area. Major Bowersox and I held in place above the two A-1s and occasionally heard an emergency locator beeper coming from the ejection site. We heard the "whoop-whoop" a few times and then it would go off. During this time, one of the A-1s took a hit, but it was not serious, so they decided to stay in the area. I had to return to the tanker one more time.

When number five and I returned from the tanker to where Donnie had gone down, the rescue chopper was holding over the Gulf of Tonkin, awaiting our assistance in proceeding to the area. Major Bowersox and I began a series of very low passes over the landing spot. I noticed a lot of people hiding behind piles of hay that had been left on the field to dry. On the second low pass, I saw a person standing in the middle of the field waving his arms. I was going very fast and very low, but I could see that he was wearing a flight suit. On this pass, I noted that the people hiding behind the hay piles were armed with rifles. Although I was tempted to tell the chopper that he should come in and attempt a pick-up, I asked Major Bowersox to verify what I had seen, and he agreed that it appeared to be a trap. The Navy A-1s also saw the villagers or soldiers in the field. When the chopper pilot heard this, he said he was aborting the rescue attempt and returning to base. The rescue attempt was called off, and we were all ordered to return to base. It was a very long and quiet flight back to Korat for Bowersox and me.

The next morning, I led a flight of four back to the area with Bill Hosmer on my wing. We neither saw nor heard anything. Our assumption was that Donnie had been captured almost immediately by the villagers because they were in close proximity to his landing site. We also assumed the beeper we heard was the North Vietnamese playing with the emergency locator beacon, or they were trying to lure us in for the kill.

In August 1965, when I returned to Okinawa, I told Donnie's wife, Sally, that the chances he was alive and a POW were very good. I was wrong. In 1973, when the POWs returned and Donnie was not among them, it became obvious that he had been killed in action. I stayed in touch with Sally Williamson, and in 1974, she told me that the Air Force had sent her some photos of an American airman lying at the feet of some North Vietnamese. The photo had appeared in a North

Vietnamese newspaper from the Vinh area, dated soon after Donnie's shoot down. She sent me a copy of the photo, and I confirmed her conclusion that it was Donnie.

Later that year, the Williamson family had a memorial service in Louisville, Kentucky, their hometown. An empty coffin was placed in a grave. Bill Hosmer and I attended the service, which was given full military honors. It was a very sad day.

In August 1989 I was very surprised to get a call from Sally Williamson asking me if I would be willing to accompany Donnie's remains from Oakland, California, to Louisville, Kentucky. The Air Force had been searching a cemetery in the area where Donnie was killed and found that it had been accidentally bombed during the war and that all the bones had been mixed together. Among the bones was a tooth that had been identified, unmistakably, as one of Donnie's.

On August 18, 1989, I arrived at the transportation office of the Oakland Army Base and was shown a copy of the x-ray identifying Donnie's tooth. I was given two small boxes containing American flags and instructed in the procedure for escorting military remains. I was to accompany the casket to Louisville, Kentucky, and before the casket was placed in the hearse, I was to drape one of the flags over it.

When I landed at Louisville, it was very late and the cargo area of the airport was closed. The owner of the mortuary picked me up in a hearse, and we went around to the back of the airport where the casket was to be delivered. What happened there was very touching.

While we waited at the back gate of the airport, we could see the headlights of a tug pulling a baggage cart toward us. There were two young men in the tug smoking, laughing, and in general, horsing around like young men do. They opened the gate and pulled the baggage cart up to the hearse so we could unload the casket. As we started to load the casket into the hearse, I remembered my instructions and halted the process while I opened one of the boxes, pulled out the American flag, and started to drape it over the casket. The laughter stopped abruptly and the mood changed. One of the boys asked who was in the casket. I told them it was the remains of Col. Donnie Williamson who was killed in action July 7, 1965, and he was being returned home for burial.

I will always remember these two young men. They stood erect, almost at attention, as we covered the casket with the flag, and slid it into the hearse. As we pulled away, I looked back and saw that they were still standing there, erect, quiet, and respectful.

The next day, Col. Donnie Williamson was once again buried with full military honors, including a fly-by of F-4 Phantoms from a nearby air base; he was also given a twenty-one gun salute. I presented one flag to Sally and the other one to Donnie's dad. I have very mixed emotions about this event because it was so hard on the family to endure this a second time. At least, this time, the casket was not empty.

016-	SFO	7321 6485			016-		7321 6485

SHIPPERS NAME AND ADDRESS

TRANSPORTATION OFFICE
HQ MIMCWA OARB
BLDG 640 DR 33
OAKLAND, CA 94626-5000
(415) 466-3332/2632

SHIPPERS ACCOUNT NUMBER
999

NOT NEGOTIABLE
AIR WAYBILL /// **UNITED AIRLINES**
(AIR CONSIGNMENT NOTE) P.O. Box 66100 Chicago, Illinois 60666
For Rates or Tracing, Call 1-800-631-1500
Copies 1, 2 and 3 of this Air Waybill are originals and have the same validity.

CONSIGNEE'S NAME AND ADDRESS

LD PEARSON & SON INC.
149 BRECKENRIDGE LANE
LOUISVILLE, KY 40207
(502) 896-0349

CONSIGNEE'S ACCOUNT NUMBER

It is agreed that the goods described herein are accepted in apparent good order and condition (except as noted) for carriage SUBJECT TO THE CONDITIONS OF CONTRACT ON THE REVERSE HEREOF. THE SHIPPER'S ATTENTION IS DRAWN OF THE NOTICE CONCERNING CARRIERS' LIMITATION OF LIABILITY. Shipper may increase such limitation of liability by declaring a higher value for carriage and paying a supplemental charge if required.

CONSIGNEE'S PHONE NUMBER

TO EXPEDITE MOVEMENT, SHIPMENT MAY BE DIVERTED TO MOTOR OR OTHER CARRIER AS PER TARIFF RULE UNLESS SHIPPER GIVES OTHER INSTRUCTIONS HEREON.

ISSUING CARRIERS AGENT NAME AND CITY

ALSO NOTIFY NAME AND ADDRESS (OPTIONAL ACCOUNTING INFORMATION)

AGENTS IATA CODE · ACCOUNT NO.

ACCOUNTING INFORMATION (SHIPPER - CHECK ONE)

DOMESTIC

AIRPORT OF DEPARTURE (ADDR OF FIRST CARRIER) AND REQUESTED ROUTING
SFO UA58 18AUG89

|XXX| FIRST FREIGHT | | GENERAL FREIGHT

ROUTING AND DESTINATION
TO: ORD BY FIRST CARRIER: UA412

TO: AIRLINE CARGO PERSONNEL

Please indicate dollar amount on the Airbill and return a copy to our office for our records in the self-addressed, stamped envelope attached. thank you.

AIRPORT OF DESTINATION
SDF

FLIGHT/DATE 58/18 FLIGHT/DATE 412/18

HANDLING INFORMATION These commodities licensed by US for ultimate destination. Diversion contrary to US law is prohibited.

GTR: V5,314,757

USAF Mortuary Office (DEHMO)
Oakland Army Base, CA 94626-5000

NO. OF PIECES RCP	GROSS WEIGHT kg lb	RATE CLASS COMMODITY ITEM NO.	CHARGEABLE WEIGHT	RATE / CHARGE	TOTAL	NATURE AND QUANTITY OF GOODS (INCL. DIMENSIONS OR VOLUME)
01	226 lbs 190	SCR0091	190	$400.00	$400.00	HUMAN REMAINS SAID TO BE: WILLIAMSON, DON I.
						ESCORT: TULLO, FRANK

Takhli—July 24, 1965

by
Paul Craw, Captain
563rd Tactical Fighter Squadron

The mission of July 24, 1965, for the 563rd Tactical Fighter Squadron (TFS) at Takhli, Thailand, was to attack an ammunition factory located 60 miles north of Hanoi. Eight F-105s, each loaded with eight 750-pound bombs with 0.25 minute fuse delay, were to attack the target, which as it turned out, was not the factory itself, but numerous underground ammunition storage sites nearby. The real stupid part of this mission was a stern warning from Secretary of Defense Robert McNamara that damage to the ammunition factory itself would result in a court-martial for the guilty individuals.

The Department of Defense apparently thought the mission was so important that they assigned a flight of four F-4C fighter interceptors to take care of any MiG threat and escort us to the target. Some escort! The F-4C pilots complained all the way to the target that they couldn't keep up with our F-105s without using their afterburners.

About the time I was ready to roll in on the target from 18,000 feet, I told the F-4Cs to return to base as there was no MiG activity and no flak in the area. After they left, we busied ourselves making pock marks on the underground storage silos, which were sturdy enough that they probably could have withstood a nuclear attack. We regrouped and headed for home, happy that we had not been shot at—or made any mistakes that would've incurred the wrath of Secretary McNamara.

The F-4Cs were probably 60 to 70

F-4C

miles in front of us, flying at 25,000 to 30,000 feet in the clouds, when all of a sudden up came the first surface-to-air (SAM) missile of the war. It was launched from one of the sites McNamara had ordered protected with a 30-mile no-fly zone. The F-4Cs were in close formation and the missile shot down two and severely damaged the other two.

When we got back to Takhli, the place was already abuzz with people planning a big mission to destroy the SAM sites. I'm sure I could have gone back that day with two F-105s and neutralized that missile site and the radar control vans once and for all. But, our squadrons were ordered to stand down from any missions on July 25 and 26, 1965, to prepare for a mass gaggle attack on the sites scheduled for July 27, 1965. This delay gave the enemy time to move large numbers of antiaircraft guns around the two SAM sites that had been targeted. Prior to this time, there had been 100 aircraft lost to small arms fire and to flak fired from 24-gun emplacements. Now, all squadrons were "standing down" (grounded) because a single SAM had been fired.

July 24 - 27, 1965

by
John Morrissey, First Lieutenant
India Flight, 12th Tactical Fighter Squadron

On the 24th of July 1965, I was airborne in the southern part of North Vietnam and monitoring the emergency guard channel on my radio when a pilot of a flight of four F-4C Phantom jets called on the radio that they had been attacked by surface-to-air missiles (SAMs) southwest of Hanoi. He reported one airplane had blown up, one airplane had no radio, and the other two were battle damaged. Our flight of F-105s was directed to counterattack immediately. We had flown about halfway through Laos when the mission was called off. This was probably a good thing, because no one knew exactly where the SAM site was located.

Within 24 hours, F-101 reconnaissance planes were sent to locate the missile sites and photograph them. On the evening of the 26th, the 101s reported they had confirmation of exactly where the SAM sites were. That night our planes were loaded up with CBUs (cluster bombs), napalm, and other munitions supposedly appropriate for attacking a SAM site. I was anxious to go, but, it wasn't going to happen.

"You know, today is the day you're supposed to go to Saigon," my flight commander, Charlie Copin, told me. I knew we always had to keep one F-105 pilot in Saigon at the headquarters of the 2nd Air Division as a resource person for the planners.

"But, boss, we're going to go north," I protested.

He was very firm. "No," he said, "you're going to Saigon."

So, I boarded a C-130 for the first leg of my trip, which would stop at Bangkok before going on to Saigon. During the layover at Don Muong Airport, I looked out at the runway and could see the KC-135 tankers scramble to launch. I thought, "Goddamn it, I'm missing the big raid!" When I finally arrived in Saigon, I went to the command post where I heard the names of all the people who had been shot down. They were very familiar to me.

THE BIRDS WERE SILVER THEN

Of all of the things that happened to me during the war, I remember missing this raid most of all. Ironically, of course, it may very well be that my absence from that event is the reason that allows me to have this memory.

Mass Gaggle

by
Lowell Peterson, Captain
Flight Surgeon, 12th Tactical Fighter Squadron

I returned from Korat to Kadena Air Base, Okinawa, on July 21, 1965, for a week of R&R. It was enjoyable to see my wife and daughter, but, the longer I was there the more anxious I became. I knew something big was coming in the air war, and I had the feeling that I needed to be involved. I heard the proclamations on the Armed Forces Radio and Television Service (AFRTS) by President Johnson and Secretary of Defense McNamara that the SAM sites were no longer sacrosanct following the July 24 attack on the F-4Cs. So, I cut my leave short, hopped a C-130 for the long flight from Okinawa to Korat, and arrived there on the evening of July 26, 1965.

I sat in on the briefings at Korat on that fateful morning of July 27, 1965, in preparation for this first mission to take out the SAM sites. It was to be a mass gaggle, involving twenty-four F-105s stationed at Korat, Thailand, and a similar number of F-105s stationed at Takhli, Thailand. A glitch overtly apparent to me and also to others, was the absence of any intelligence photos of the SAM sites. We were assured the F-101 photo reconnaissance planes had obtained fresh photos, but by the time of the launch, we had not received any.

I remember, after the preflight briefing, sitting down with Percy (Capt. Robert Purcell) and having a lighthearted talk. Percy always had a smile and a twinkle in his dark eyes, which were protected by a tangle of heavy dark eyebrows. He had an equally bushy head of dark hair, and the required mustache of the combat fighter pilot. He reminded me of Lee Trevino, the golfer. Percy had a "what-the-hell" attitude, and was often heard to say, "Give me my airplane and my orders and turn me loose." Percy also had a history of ulcers. I probably could theorize that all of his suppressed fears and anxieties were channeled to his stomach, but Percy never gave me the impression that anything bothered him. I had been supplying him with antacid tablets by the gross for all of the time I had known him, such that they became widely known as "Percy Pills". Fortunately, he had not had any major complication of his affliction that ever kept him from flying.

That morning he said to me, "Doc, I think I've got it licked; my ulcers haven't acted up in several weeks now. Thanks for keeping me in the air."

I joked with him and told him that maybe he was just drinking a better brand of gin. His loud laughter rattled the boards in the rickety wooden operations building, which we called our Base-Ops.

The control tower was the best place to watch a flightline takeoff, and there was no other place I wanted to be on July 27, 1965. The control tower operator, a master sergeant, was surprised to see me there and assumed that I was just checking him out on a routine duty station check. We were talking when suddenly twenty-four airplanes lit off their black powder smoke canisters simultaneously and ignited their engines. The startled master sergeant jumped off his feet in amazement and exclaimed, "Holy shit!" He had never seen more than two flights of four planes start up and prepare to launch at any one time, and they always started engines with generators rather than black powder cannisters.

The next voice I heard was across the radio and was noticeably calmer, "This is Dogwood Lead. Permission to taxi with flight of four."

The air traffic controller stuttered, "Yes, sir, Dogwood Lead—proceed to runway arming area and hold."

"Roger," was the reply. Each flight of four made the same call, and then taxied in tandem, leaving their parking spots on cue, in an absolutely perfect formation that was as precise as a John Philip Sousa march. As they advanced to the end of the runway, I uttered a silent prayer for their safe return.

The takeoff of two F-105s side-by-side is something to behold—taxiing into position, holding, releasing brakes, slowly advancing to full power, lighting afterburners, accelerating, spitting fire out of the tailpipe, increasing speed down the runway, rotating, and lifting off. Although it was a thrill of a lifetime for me to be a part of this, I knew the gravity of the situation as well. It was time for me to go back, get my ambulances and crews on alert, and bring them to the flightline. Col. Robert Fair, the Operations Officer, told me after the launch that he expected 25- to 40-percent airplane losses on this mission. As soon as the planes left, he ordered the taxiways cleared with ground sweepers because he believed we were going to have to recover battle damaged airplanes, several at a time, not only on the runway but on taxiways as well. Bob Fair had a good head on his shoulders, and it was working overtime on July 27, 1965.

As I listened to the radio with Colonel Fair at Operations, we heard no reports on our assigned channel until the flights cleared the target and were heading home. The initial report was in code indicating the mission was successful but the subsequent transmissions were less than enthusiastic. Colonel Fair requested a casualty report and received some excited replies that there had been losses, referring to the pilots that had been shot down by their call-signs, and that rescue operations were underway. I soon found out that Percy had been shot down, but a chute had not been seen. His fate was unknown but it was doubted that he had survived. Frank Tullo—call sign: Dogwood Two—was also shot down and rescue efforts were reported to be underway. It was soon reported that shortly after leaving the target area, McConnell Squadron Commander Major Farr flew up to take visual inspection of Bill (Bart) Bartholomou's plane, which had suffered severe battle damage. Just at that time, Bart's plane lost control and pitched directly into Major Farr's plane, knocking down both planes and killing Major Farr instantly. Bart was able to bail out, but his chute "streamered", failing to open, and he was killed. Korat and Takhli lost six airplanes that day.

The entire mission frayed the nerves of the pilots, and they were glad to get back on friendly, solid ground. Lieut. Chuck Large of Juliett Flight, one of my "hooch" mates, said that was the closest he had ever come to "pranging-in" and "buying the farm" (crashing and dying). He said that as he pulled off the target, juking around to avoid other planes and the guns firing at him, he was in a tight turn and was sure his tail barely missed scraping the ground. It was a miracle that more mid-air collisions and more combat losses did not occur that day.

That evening the pre-mission intelligence photos finally arrived at Korat. It was soon obvious that what our pilots had attacked was not a SAM missile site at all but just telephone poles painted white with an active radar unit sitting out in the open without camouflage. The United States Air Force pilots had been the victims of a major sting operation by the North Vietnamese. We were all depressed, and angry.

Takhli—July 27, 1965

by
Paul Craw, Captain
563rd Tactical Fighter Squadron

The plan as presented to us from the Department of Defense and the chain of command was to simultaneously hit both targeted SAM sites on July 27, 1965. The F-105 squadrons from Korat, Thailand, were to hit the eastern site going north and our Takhli squadrons were to hit the western site going south. The ordnance was to be napalm and cluster antipersonnel bombs (CBUs). The CBUs that we had at that time would lay only a foot-wide swath for several thousand feet. Their use was not what I would call a worthwhile venture for this type of target.

Flight spacing was two minutes between flights on the target. Jack Brown, the Takhli commander, led the first flight loaded with CBUs, E. W. Harris led the second flight carrying napalm, and I, Paul Craw, led the third flight also carrying napalm. The Takhli group proceeded north to Yen Bai and then down the Red River Valley on the deck at low altitude. It was mid-afternoon—humid, hazy, and calm. The scenery was rather beautiful with all the farms, grass-roofed huts, and banana trees.

Will Koenitzer still has a copy of the frag (official order) for the mission and notes that our time-on-target (TOT) was 0700 Zulu (Greenwich mean time), which translates to 1400 hours Hanoi time and 1300 hours Korat and Takhli time.

When we arrived at the intersection of the Red and Black Rivers, just short of the target, I was at 500 knots and 100 feet altitude above ground level, perfectly lined up on the missile. My napalm release should have resulted in a sure kill. Jack Redmond, who was number four in one of the Takhli flights, recalled that when he looked at the target area, he saw nothing but smoke and a solid wall of ground fire. Just beyond the target, I called for afterburners and started a right turn to get back across the Black River.

Walt Kosko, Jack Brown's number two man, took a hit over the target. Jack was trying to encourage Walt to stay with the airplane until he got across the river prior to ejecting. He didn't quite make it. He landed in the river, and was dragged down by his chute and drowned. As I was turning to the right off target with my burner cooking, Sparky started yelling to me, "Hudson lead, get out, you're on fire!".

I knew I was not on fire and answered back, "Negative, negative, negative." You don't tell someone to eject from the aircraft just because it is on fire, especially if you are within ten miles of chopper pickup territory. I looked in the rearview mirror and picked out the aircraft of my number two man, Kile Berg. All I could see was the radome nose with the rest of the plane engulfed in fire. I saw the nose come up just before the aircraft rolled to the right and splashed. Marty Case, the number four man did not see Kile get out of the aircraft, but as it turned out, he had ejected safely and was picked up by the bad guys within five minutes. We did not know he was a POW until almost two years later. The rest of us turned around and headed for home.

My Last Combat Flight

by
Jim Sandin, First Lieutenant
Kilo Flight, 12th Tactical Fighter Squadron

My last flight of the Vietnam War was on July 27, 1965. The North Vietnamese had been allowed to build multiple surface-to-air missile (SAM) sites without any U.S. interference. The enemy finally launched a SAM attack on four F-4Cs exiting a target area near Hanoi, resulting in the loss of two planes. U.S. Secretary of Defense Robert McNamara told the world the United States would respond to this attack, erasing all doubts that the SAM sites were still off limits.

Our flight, led by Major Bowersox, was assigned to attack a support area about thirty-five miles west of Hanoi as part of a large-scale attack on multiple targets, including the SAM sites. As we crossed into North Vietnam, we were flying fifty feet above the valley floor at about 400 knots. There were rocky outcroppings all along the Red River Valley reaching to heights of 150 feet, so we had to climb to a little higher altitude every once in awhile to get above them. I noted that while we were at the higher altitude, the flak bursts from the North Vietnamese antiaircraft guns were actually below us. The North Vietnamese had put up telephone poles painted white as SAM decoys and had buried the front supports for the 88-millimeter antiaircraft guns so that the shells would explode at a minimum of fifty feet above the ground instead of their usual 120-foot minimum burst altitude. That's the reason we saw flak below us when we climbed to 150 feet above ground level.

On our way into the target area, radio transmissions from flights preceding us were reporting several aircraft getting hit and pilots bailing out. As I was leaving the target area after expending my ordnance, a tracer bullet went under my right wing, followed by another one under my left wing. Although I was doing 450 knots at fifty feet and trailing the rest of the flight in the number four position, I went into afterburner to get out of there. The auxiliary hydraulic system pump surged before the burner lit, and I mistakenly thought the engine was surging and that one of those tracers had gone up my tailpipe. I reasoned that it wasn't a good idea to be in afterburner, dumping extra fuel into the engine area, which would just make me burn faster. I came out of afterburner, and then realized that I had no fire-light indicator and the airplane was running smoothly. I went back into afterburner and got up to about 520 knots, quickly overtaking Major Bowersox and the rest of the flight as we headed back to base.

Because my helmet apparently did not fit properly, and due to the high decibel level in the airplane, I developed an 80 percent loss of hearing in my right ear, which disqualified me for flight status. I was sent back to Kadena Air Force Base and, after a couple of weeks, my hearing returned.

> *Author's Note: I did an extensive research project on the noise problem of the F-105, including decibel readings from the cockpit during static test run-ups. The problem was primarily the high-frequency generator noise and not the noise of the jet engines. I wrote this up and submitted it to headquarters along with a solution to the problem—better ear protection with silicone ear pads in the helmets to fit the ears smoothly and keep out unwanted noise. Although nobody listened initially, eventually my recommendation was accepted and implemented.*

Korat—July 27, 1965

by

Bill Hosmer, Major

Flight Commander, Lima Flight, 12th Tactical Fighter Squadron

Secretary of Defense Robert McNamara and President Johnson's adminis-tration did not allow us to attain air superiority over the North Vietnamese, and we, as pilots, were helpless to change the course of events. Then, at the end of July 1965, in response to the first firing and downing of American aircraft by SAM missiles by the North Vietnamese, operation Iron Hand was ordered and initiated.

My part of the mission on July 27, 1965, was to lead an eight-ship flight to the target and wipe out anything left standing after the initial assault on the SAM sites and the supporting barracks areas. We would arrive on target about fifteen minutes after everybody else. We were to fly below one thousand feet in the target area to avoid being targeted by the SAMs. Frank Tullo, Al "Andy" Anderson, and Norlan "Bob" Daughtery were in my four-ship flight. Charlie Copin led the other four ships with Gene Frank, Matt Kelch, and George Bogert on his wing.

Robert "Percy" Purcell was our weapons officer. During the night prior to the raid, he had supervised the mixing and loading of a new kind of napalm that had been designated to be used on this mission. On the morning of the 27th, he asked me, "Who am I flying with?"

I said, "Percy, you've been up all night, I don't think you should fly today."

He said, "I mixed it, I want to drop it."

I suggested that he speak to the squadron commander, Col. Chuck Reed. He did, and that day he flew as a wingman with Colonel Reed.

Frank Tullo and others have their own stories about what happened that day, but from my cockpit, it went like this:

We came in low and fast and delivered our ordnance on the target area while the whole sky was lighting up with flak burst and tracer bullets. It looked like a 4th of July fireworks extravaganza gone bad, where everything exploded at once. As we jinked and juked different directions to avoid the worst of the flak and get out of there, my number two man, Frank Tullo, was hit and was on fire. After some excited radio exchanges encouraging Frank to bail out before his plane blew up, he ejected. I told Al to take the rest of the element up high, and I would stay low with Frank during his descent in the chute. I told Charlie to go back to the tankers to take on fuel so his flight could relieve us when we got to "Bingo" fuel (the amount required to return to base). Charlie informed me the tankers were all gone, so I told him to take his flight and return to base at Korat.

Another flight of Thuds (F-105s) from Takhli did take on fuel before the tankers left, and they were capping over one of their own guys who had been shot down just south of Frank. I asked them for possible relief, since I was running low on fuel, and got a welcome affirmative. I told them I had voice contact with Frank, and that I would describe where he was. They were still about thirty miles away, and before I had to split, I needed to talk fast and accurately so they could pinpoint Frank's location. I described the terrain in the foothills of the mountains in rapid and graphic terms, saying that the area resembled the most important part of the female anatomy. They said that they had it in sight. When I had a visual on them, and they had voice contact with Frank, I headed for Udorn, Thailand, which was the closest recovery base.

I waited at Udorn and listened in at the communications center, which was monitoring the rescue effort. It took a long time, but we finally got the word that Frank, was in fact, rescued. That made me feel great! By that time, our flight had been refueled, so we left Udorn and flew to Korat. I walked to the Operations building, all tired out and needing a drink.

Ralph Bowersox met me, and said, "It looks like you did a good job with Frank, but we don't think Percy made it."

I broke down, not knowing until that minute that he had been bagged (shot down). We were unable to determine whether Percy had been captured or killed in action.

Charlie Copin related, "Percy's wing got shot off and he flipped upside down." No one saw him eject, and no one saw a chute. We had only faint hope for his survival.

We had a memorial service for Percy at the Korat Air Force Base chapel. After that, I sent Frank Tullo back to Okinawa with Percy's foot locker, as I got ready for our next try at the SAMs. I did not think Frank should be sent north again after what he had just been through. Colonel Reed told Frank to tell Marion Purcell it was likely Percy had been killed in action and to tell Sally Williamson her husband, Don (shot down earlier in July), was likely a POW (prisoner of war). It turned out that just the opposite was true. Such is the tragedy of war.

A couple of weeks later, Bob Daughtery, another of my wingmen from that fateful day at the end of July, was bagged during an attack on the Than Hoa Bridge. When I saw him after the war, he told me his arms were useless after suffering the many breaks, which occurred during his ejection. When he reached the Hanoi Hilton, he was lying in a holding area for new POWs and saw, scratched on a wall, "Percy, 7/27". He thought to himself, "My God, I'm the only one in the world who knows Percy is alive, and I can't do a thing about it."

Dogwood Two

by
Frank Tullo, Captain
Lima Flight, 12th Tactical Fighter Squadron

On the morning of July 27, 1965, I was told by my squadron commander to report to Operations to plan the day's missions. Although this was my assigned task as the targets and navigation officer, target planning was usually done the evening before a strike. When I arrived at Operations and looked at the frag order (daily mission orders from 2nd Air Division headquarters in Saigon), I was surprised to see the surface-to-air missile (SAM) sites were not the only targets planned. The Chiefs of Staff had decided that since they were sending air attacks into the 30-mile circle around Hanoi, they would also order strikes at other vulnerable targets, such as barrack areas and command and control centers.

This was to be a maximum effort, and all available and airworthy aircraft were fragged for the mission. I was assigned to an aircraft that had been configured to fly back to Okinawa for scheduled maintenance. It had a large, 600-gallon fuel tank on the centerline station under the fuselage. The crew chief did not have time to de-fuel the tank and load rockets or bombs on that station, so I was going to have to take off with the tank still on the aircraft. As a result, the only armament I had was two pods of rockets on the outboard wing stations. Each of the other aircraft in the flight carried two outboard fuel tanks, either CBUs (Cluster Bombs) or napalm, plus two pods of seventeen 2.75-inch rockets.

On the afternoon of July 27th, forty-eight U.S. Air Force F-105s took off from two bases at Korat and Takhli, Thailand, topping off their fuel tanks from KC-135 tankers over eastern Thailand before heading for their targets. All targets were to be approached at low altitude, one hundred feet above ground level. Our briefings said that we could expect extremely heavy flak and SAM missile firings and that MiGs would likely be active in the area.

Because of my plane's unusual configuration, our flight of four F-105s turned off to the south after takeoff so I could fly over our bomb jettison area, a designated drop site, and get rid of the 600-gallon tank attached to my aircraft. After jettisoning the tank the flight to the tankers was uneventful, and we took on a full load of fuel before proceeding to the target area.

I was number two in a flight of four led by one of my favorite pilots and a good friend, Maj. Bill Hosmer. We had flown many combat and training flights together, and I felt bulletproof when I was on his wing. The second flight of four in our group of eight was led by Maj. Charlie Copin. Our mission was to take off from Korat, Thailand, reconnoiter each of the SAM sites that were to be hit that day, and attack any equipment that had survived strikes by aircraft that had preceded us to the target.

I was feeling very confident, as I was with Hosmer and we had done this many times before. When we were close enough to the target area to switch to the combat radio frequency of the day, we began to hear radio calls spelling out that the defenses were far greater than expected, and that a number of aircraft had already been hit and gone down. We could clearly hear emergency beacons, which automatically sound whenever a pilot ejects from his airplane.

We were very low, probably three hundred feet or lower, as we entered the 30-mile circle and raced northward toward our first SAM target just south of the center of the city of Hanoi. We normally flew the aircraft unpressurized once we entered the combat zone, and I can clearly remember smelling gunpowder from the outside air. This amount of antiaircraft fire was something we had never encountered, and it produced a thick layer of black smoke hanging two hundred feet above the city. The gunners picked up our approach and were feverishly firing as we flashed by. For this Catholic boy from Chicago, it was my idea of what hell must be like.

With the city of Hanoi on the horizon, we could see our SAM target. Dogwood Lead (Major Hosmer) called out that he had the target in sight and made a slight heading correction to begin the attack. I was about one hundred feet off his right wing. That call was followed immediately by his announcement that he thought the enemy had salvoed all of the missiles from the SAM site because of the amount of smoke and fire coming from the general direction of the site. What he did not know then—but found out an instant later—was that the smoke and fire were from an unbelievable number of antiaircraft guns placed all around what was once a SAM site but now was simply a flak trap. The North Vietnamese had placed heavy artillery all around a fake SAM site and lured us into range of their guns as cannon fodder.

Dogwood Lead made a hard left turn to avoid the antiaircraft fire, but we were so close and going so fast that we still ended up flying over the target area. I looked down as we passed over the site and could see a number of gun emplacements with four gun barrels firing from a single platform, fire spitting from every barrel. As we emerged from the smoke and antiaircraft fire, I was immediately aware of a large red light on my instrument panel that said "Fire". Since I had no other indications that I had been hit, I searched the other engine instruments in my cockpit for signs that might confirm the fire light. Dogwood Three soon confirmed my worst fears. I was on fire! Dogwood Lead instantly confirmed Dogwood Three's report.

My aircraft seemed to be flying well and responding to my inputs, so I felt no great threat at the moment. Dogwood Lead told me to jettison my external load, which I did quickly, feeling sheepish that I did not think of it myself. This lightened the aircraft and removed the drag, but I was soon advised by someone in the flight that the fire was getting larger. This convinced me that I should try to find a safe place to eject if the situation deteriorated further. Our flight was heading west at this time, and I spotted a mountain in the distance. Our training had taught us to, "seek high, rugged terrain over which to eject." This would give me the greatest chance of being rescued before the North Vietnamese could capture me. I set a course toward the mountain west of Hanoi, and Hosmer told me to take the lead. Of course, I was hoping the fire would go out and I would be able to make it back to my home base, but this was not in the cards. I began to hear muffled explosions. We were very low, going very fast, and still being fired on by gunners as we approached the edge of Hanoi. Then things really started to go wrong. The air turbine motor, which produces electrical power for the instruments, quit working, and as a result I started losing all of my standard instruments, although I still had a standby airspeed indicator. It was pegged at 400 knots, which is as high as it goes. I made a call to Dogwood Lead that "everything is turning to shit," and immediately began to look for some place to eject. I was not going to make it to the mountain, but there was a river ahead, and just beyond that, a very thick jungle or undergrowth. I headed for this but soon felt the nose of the aircraft drop slightly. When I pulled the control stick back to raise the nose of the aircraft, it failed to respond. I had to eject now!

I reached for the ejection handles on either side of the seat and pulled them up. The canopy blew clear of the aircraft, the ejection triggers were exposed, and my elbows were automatically locked inside the seat to avoid injury at bail out. The roar of the wind rushing past the open cockpit was deafening. I hesitated for a second or two, and then I squeezed the triggers.

What occurred next was so unbelievably violent that my mind refuses to remember it as being real. In the flash of a moment, my seat belt and shoulder harness were opened, and I was pushed out of the ejection seat by an apparatus called the "butt-slapper," which also pulls the D-ring on the parachute, causing it to open automatically. The force of the wind stream was great enough to rip my helmet off, even though I had the chin strap fastened and had an oxygen mask strapped to my helmet covering my face.

My first memory after "punching out" (ejecting) was that I was in the chute and everything was quiet and serene. All I could hear were the distant muffled engine noises of my flight disappearing to the west. When I looked up to check the parachute, I realized I could only see out of my right eye. When my helmet was torn from my head, the oxygen mask had made a deep cut over my left eye, and a flap of skin, including my left eyebrow, was covering the eye and filling it with blood. I could have cared less! I was happy just to be alive.

During this time, I experienced a strange phenomenon: I felt I was inside my own head looking through two holes that were my eyes; as if I was looking through a gun barrel. I was in the parachute for just a few seconds, but I did see the city of Hanoi behind me and what looked like a small farmhouse, with some cleared fields around it, just a mile or so to the west. I looked down and could tell exactly where I would land. I hit the ground hard and immediately gathered my chute and stuffed it under some brush. I was in a very thick undergrowth of elephant grass with an occasional large bush or tree visible here and there. It was great cover. I felt I was invisible from anyone more than ten feet away. I pulled out my emergency radio, turned it on, and immediately heard Dogwood Lead calling me. I responded, telling him I was okay, and in a great place for a rescue, but that I had lost my cigarettes during the ejection. I realized that I would have to go through this experience without a smoke! When my flight got close enough for me to see them again, the antiaircraft guns to the east of my position began firing. The closer Dogwood flight came, the more intense the fire, and I could hear shrapnel and shells cutting into the grass around me. I told the flight that they should move away, farther west. Dogwood Lead told me he knew about where I was, and he would make the required calls to start the rescue attempt. He also told me he was low on fuel and had been ordered to leave the area. He said, "Your ordeal may be an all-nighter."

It became very quiet, and I began to perceive every noise as a threat. I realized that I was breathing as shallowly as I could to make as little noise as possible. After bandaging the cut above my eye, I tried to keep myself busy by sorting through the emergency equipment in my vest and in the seat pack from the ejection seat. It was then I realized I had not pulled the lanyard on the emergency seat pack after ejection. (Pulling the lanyard opens the seat pack and allows a fifty-foot cord to drop; this cord has an emergency equipment bag at the twenty-five foot level with many necessary items for escape and evasion. At the fifty-foot level at the end of the cord, there is a yellow, one-man, self-inflating life raft dinghy.)

I pulled the lanyard and the dinghy began to inflate with a very loud rushing air noise that I was sure everybody in North Vietnam could hear. I pulled out my survival knife and jumped on the dinghy, stabbing it, trying to deflate it. To my surprise, my first two stabs resulted in the knife just bouncing off the tough material. My third thrust punctured the dinghy, and I hurriedly hid it under some brush. I have often wondered what a North Vietnamese soldier would have thought if he had come upon me at the moment I was "killing" my dinghy!

After ten or fifteen minutes I heard the unmistakable sound of more F-105s, and I turned my radio on, calling, in the clear, to any F-105s over North Vietnam. I was answered by a flight of two Thuds (105s) which were near but not able to help in any way, except to tell the command post that I was still talking. They made a sweep over my position, drew some flak, and asked me to "pop some smoke" (light a smoke bomb flare), which I refused to do because it would give away my position to the enemy. They told me there were some buses unloading soldiers south of my position and that I would possibly be getting some visitors real soon. I asked about the rescue attempt and they assured me it was ongoing and that I should be patient.

After being on the ground for about a half an hour, I heard the sound of engines. Two propeller-driven aircraft, which I recognized as A-1s, used by the Navy as rescue aircraft, were inbound to my position. I called them on the radio and they identified themselves as Canasta Flight. They took directions from me until they were right over my position. They also started to draw fire from the anti-aircraft sites to the east and from the troops down in the valley. I looked up and told Canasta Lead that I was looking right straight up at his wing. He responded by saying that he had my position and knew exactly where I was. This was very reassuring. (Years later, Canasta Lead admitted to me that he did not see me, but wanted to ease my mind.) Because of heavy ground fire, Canasta Flight was soon ordered out of the area, but as they left, they said they would be back with a rescue helicopter.

For the next two-and-a-half hours, I did everything in my power to be invisible and quiet. I did not hear movement of the North Vietnamese soldiers who were searching for me, but I could hear their voices as they hacked their way through the underbrush. I also heard their gunfire. The gunfire was the worst of all. It would start with one or two shots but almost instantly would crescendo into an enormous amount of firing, accompanied by a lot of yelling. You can imagine how frightened I was. Their indiscriminate firing apparently was a normal procedure they used when looking for a pilot hiding in the brush. I soon became aware they were moving north in the valley toward my position. They came very close, and I got a glimpse of a uniformed soldier about one hundred feet away. I was in the thickest undercover in the valley, and I guess the steepness of the terrain and the thick underbrush discouraged them, because they began to move west.

I had been on the ground approximately three hours when I again began to hear the sound of engines. It was Canasta Flight, and they told me by radio that they had a helicopter. Before I knew it, Canasta was over me and drawing fire from the troops in the valley. Then things started happening very quickly. I talked to the helicopter pilot and directed him to my position. As the rescue chopper got close to me, I fired two small rescue flares, which he said he did not see. I then fired off two red smoke flares, which he also did not see. Finally, in desperation, I fired six tracer bullets which I had loaded into my sidearm, a .38-caliber revolver. These he saw very clearly and came straight in, with a sling hanging below the chopper. The helicopter was a CH3-C, a cargo version of the combat choppers that would become known as "Jolly Green Giants" later in the war. As I found out, this was the first combat pickup by this type of aircraft. Capt. George Martin, piloting the chopper, had chosen the call sign "Jolly Green" and the name stuck.

I stowed my radio back into my vest and grabbed the chopper's sling called a horse collar, which it resembled, wrapping it under my armpits. I could see the helicopter crew chief working the cable as he began to hoist me upward. When I was about six or seven feet above the ground, the hoist stopped and I dangled there just above the undergrowth. I looked up at the crew chief and gave him the thumbs-up sign. He was working on the hoist, which obviously was jammed. This hoist had been quickly jury-rigged because this helicopter, originally configured as a cargo aircraft, had no hoist for lifting downed pilots. At this point, the helicopter pilot, who was taking fire from the troops in the valley, decided that I was clear of the jungle and began pulling away to depart the area. Unfortunately, I wasn't completely clear and I was pulled through some bushes and hit the side of a very large tree.

For the next twenty minutes, I hung in the sling as the chopper circled the valley trying to pull me up. I did not look down very often, because every time I did, I realized how high I was, and because I also could see white puffs of smoke from the North Vietnamese gunfire. After awhile, the crew chief lowered a rope to me and signaled me to tie it to the sling. The sling fits tightly under the arms and was cutting off circulation to my hands, which were now numb from the tension. Tying that rope to the sling was probably going to be the last thing I could possibly do before I completely lost feeling in my hands, which already felt like boxing gloves. They pulled me up about five or six feet with the rope, but then could not pull me any higher because of the downwash from the chopper blades. Being pulled up a bit, however, created a big loop in the original cable, and I was able to put my foot in the loop and release some of the pressure on my armpits.

I realized the chopper was no longer circling, but going somewhere. It was heading toward the small farmhouse that I had seen when I was in the parachute. As we approached the field in front of the house, I realized that if someone was there with a gun, I was a sitting duck. As we approached the freshly-plowed field, I saw a brightly colored banty rooster scoot across the field. Captain Martin set me down gently in the field and maneuvered to land next to me. I kept as low as possible with my eye on the house. As the helicopter landed, I got up and started running for the entrance side of the aircraft. Just as I reached the chopper, I heard an automatic weapon begin firing from the farmhouse. I dove into the plane, and as I lay on the deck, I could hear the engines roar at takeoff power, and when I looked forward to the cockpit, both pilots had their heads down as low as possible. We made a successful takeoff, but everyone in the plane heard and felt the helicopter taking hits.

The chopper climbed and a medic began to administer to me. I noticed he had an Air Force uniform on, and I asked him if this was an Air Force chopper.

He answered, "Yeh, this is a CH3-C that's just been assigned to Thailand."

As we climbed to altitude, I became very cold and realized that my entire flight suit was drenched through with sweat. I began to shake uncontrollably. The crew did everything they could to make me comfortable, including giving me a much-needed cigarette. I am sure the shakes were due as much to stress as they were to the cold air.

The chopper could not make it back to Thailand because of a lack of fuel and the onset of darkness. Instead, we landed on a hilltop controlled by Hmong tribesmen in Laos, called Lima Site Number 36. This was a small outpost of friendly land surrounded by Viet Cong, North Vietnamese, and Communist Pathet Lao forces. The landing zone was surrounded by markers of burning smudge pots. We were greeted by friendly faces, and when I got out of the chopper, I was welcomed by an American in civilian clothes (CIA operative) who had a full bottle of Whitehorse Scotch, which I immediately put to my lips for a liberal taste.

I spent the night in a fortified bunker with the helicopter crew. We were fed and entertained by the American men who were stationed there and by the Laotians who were defending the fort against the Vietnamese and Pathet Lao. During the evening, we heard the unmistakable sound of incoming mortars, and the bunker immediately emptied, leaving the helicopter crew and me alone. We occasionally would look out slit holes in the bunker and see tracer bullets crossing above us.

The next morning, I was asked what my call sign was. This surprised me, since I was sure everyone knew whom they had rescued. I responded, Dogwood Two. A command ship was flying above Lima Site Number 36 making sure who had been rescued, because there had been six 105s shot down that day. I did not know of the other shoot downs until that very moment. Later that morning, a Platis Porter airplane landed on the five-hundred-foot airstrip, and I got on board for the flight to Vientiane, the capital of Laos. When I arrived in Vientiane, I was whisked away by two Air Force officers for debriefing. These two gentlemen kept insisting that I was not telling them everything I knew. I told them that I saw very little when I was on the ground because I was trying to be invisible, but they kept debriefing me for over an hour.

A "bird" Colonel came into the room and told the two officers that Gen. Hunter Harris, the four-star commander of the Pacific Air Forces, was at the officers club and wanted to talk to me. Although I was glad to get away from the debriefers, I was very nervous about presenting myself to a four-star general in the condition I was in at that moment. Remember, I had spent over three hours on the ground in North Vietnam and the rest of the night on the dirt floor of a bunker in Laos. I had a bandage over my left eye, my flight suit had blood spots on it and was stained white from sweat, and I had not shaved for a couple of days.

I was escorted into the largest room of the Officers Club at Vientiane. There, at the head of a huge U-shaped group of tables, was Gen. Hunter Harris. There were at least thirty officers from all U.S. military services, and from Laos. All were dressed very properly, having lunch with the General. At his insistence, I was seated next to him so we could talk. He asked me all kinds of questions about my experience. I learned that I was the only pilot to be rescued the day before. He wanted to know what I felt was the reason for the extreme losses. I told him the SAM site target was a flak trap designed to attract the striking aircraft into a turkey shoot. I also expressed my opinion that our tactics at low level with such a large number of aircraft were flawed. Then, after making sure I had something to eat and drink, he asked if there was something he could do for me. I asked him if he could get me back to my squadron at Korat. He told the Colonel to make sure that I was on his plane, because that was where he was going next.

Gen. Hunter Harris had a KC-135 with his four stars on the side of the aircraft fuselage behind the cockpit. The airplane was polished to a luster I had never seen before. I was ushered aboard and into the cockpit, where I sat in an extra seat during the entire flight to Korat. The General, who was flying the airplane, said he hoped there would be some fighters that needed fuel so he could refuel them, but there were no takers that day.

We landed at Korat, and as we taxied in, I noticed a band playing where the airplane was to park. I slipped out of the cockpit and tried to be inconspicuous, but when the General came out of the cockpit and the boarding door opened, he asked where I was. To my surprise, and I am sure to the even greater surprise of all those outside waiting for the General to emerge, he insisted that I go out first. When my squadron mates saw me come out of the aircraft, they rushed forward to greet me at the bottom of the stairs and whisked me off for some much-needed conversation. It was suggested that I go take a shower and change clothes, because I "smelled like a goat."

The reunion was very emotional. When everything settled down and the General had left, most of the squadron sat around and compared notes on what had happened the day before. Korat had lost four F-105s and Takhli had lost two. Among those lost from Korat was a very close friend, Bob "Percy" Purcell, a member of Lima Flight, the flight that Hosmer commanded. He became a POW for the next seven-and-one-half years. Lima Flight hooch had two empty beds the night before I returned. My first two days as a captain had been very eventful, to say the least (I had pinned on my captain's bars at the Officers Club on the evening of July 26, 1965, to a chorus of toasts from my squadron mates).

From that day forward, I began a quest to find the pilots of Canasta Flight who had played such a pivitol role in my recovery. I kept in close contact with George Martin, the chopper pilot, but I had lost the opportunity to thank the members of Canasta Flight, because their ship had rotated out of the Gulf of Tonkin shortly after my shoot down. For the next twenty-eight years, I kept asking any Navy or Marine pilot I ran into if they knew what carrier or squadron Canasta Flight was on, but to no avail. Finally, in late 1993, I was casually talking to an ex-Marine helicopter pilot and mentioned the incident. He told me it was the carrier *Midway* and VA25 was the squadron. He also told me there was a publication called, *The Hook*, a magazine for Navy pilots that could probably help me locate them. I contacted *The Hook*, and they suggested that I put an ad in their locator section and maybe someone would respond. Two days later, I was called by someone from the staff at the magazine who saw my ad and knew who the pilots were and how I could locate them. That same day, I was speaking with Canasta Lead, Ed Greathouse, the pilot who had helped rescue me. He was pleasantly surprised that I had never given up hope of finding the pilots who were instrumental in my rescue. We talked for almost an hour comparing notes, and then made plans to meet in Houston, Texas, before the year's end. It took a few days to get in touch with Canasta Two, Holt Livesay, but we finally talked on the phone and recounted our impressions of that day in North Vietnam.

THE BIRDS WERE SILVER THEN

On July 27, 1995, thirty years to the day after that eventful day, a meeting took place in Austin, Texas, at the home of Ed Greathouse, with Canasta Lead (Ed), Canasta Two (Holt), Jolly Green One (George), and Dogwood Two (Frank Tullo). Our wives met for the first time and listened to the story told many different ways from the viewpoints of the four pilots. Needless to say, it got emotional at times. We all reconvened again in Dayton, Ohio, on July 27, 2005, for a 40-year reunion where Dogwood Lead, Bill Hosmer, and the author of this book also joined us.

I stand in awe of the brave Air Force and Navy pilots and crew who rescued me, and I will be eternally grateful to all of these men who risked their lives to save mine.

Canasta Flight

by
Holt Livesay, Ensign
VA-25 Squadron, *USS Midway*, U.S. Navy

I joined squadron VA-25 on board the *USS Midway* in March 1965, and was the only Ensign aviator in the entire carrier air wing. I flew the Douglas A1-H and A1-J Skyraider aircraft. Its slang designation was the "Spad", because it was somewhat antiquated and begged comparison with the old Spad planes of World War I. (I remember being in the Ready Room aboard ship one evening when our skipper, commanding officer Capt. Harry Ettinger, received a copy of WWI ace Capt. Eddie Rickenbacker's book, signed by the author with the inscription, "To one old Spad driver from another.")

The Wright R3350-WD engine produced 2,800 horsepower for the large single propeller which allowed the airplane to carry a huge armament and fuel load capacity. Flying conservatively, we could cut fuel consumption to 400 pounds per hour, and therefore could be airborne for about as long as we could stand to sit in the thing. It was originally designed as a close-air-support dive bomber. Our cruising speed was 160 knots, but we could exceed 300 knots in a dive.

We spent many hours in armed reconnaissance over Vietnam, flying day and night looking for targets of opportunity. We would typically launch from the carrier $1\frac{1}{2}$ hours prior to the jet launches to allow us time to get to the target area. After the jet aircraft and our A-1s coordinated our attack on the primary target, the jets would return to the carrier while we did several more hours of reconnaissance work. That's why, when we talked to the jet jockeys, we talked in terms of combat hours while they wanted to count combat missions.

My squadron mates and I flew close air support over U.S. ground forces that were under attack at various outposts. However, one of our primary missions was Rescue Combat Air Patrol (RESCAP) because we had the armament and the fuel capacity to hang around over an area for long periods of time.

The aircraft carrier *USS Midway* entered the Tonkin Gulf on April 10, 1965, and began combat operations which continued until June 27, 1965, when we were relieved and sent to Yokuska, Japan, for an enjoyable period of R&R. While we were in Japan, we heard about the new surface-to-air missiles (SAMs) the North Vietnamese were installing around the countryside, and we saw photographs of them taken by reconnaissance aircraft. Navy pilots were ordered to stay outside a fifteen-mile radius of the SAM sites, but even I could reason that if we allowed the Vietnamese to build one and then go thirty miles from the center and build another, they would soon have all of North Vietnam covered by missile circles that we were not allowed to enter.

We departed Japan in mid-July and were back on station in the Tonkin Gulf on July 23, 1965. On July 27, 1965, I was scheduled for an 11 a.m. launch to fly wing position on Lt. Comdr. Hal Gray for a RESCAP combat air patrol mission. Lieutenant Commander Gray's engine began running rough about one hundred miles from the ship, forcing him to return. I held in the vicinity of the ship until Lt. Comdr. Ed Greathouse could launch as my new flight leader. After joining up with Ed, we flew to an area off the North Vietnamese coast between the cities of Vinh and Than Hoa . A U.S. HU-16 amphibious aircraft was also sent to the area for the possibility of water rescue.

About 4 p.m. we received a call that an Air Force pilot was down. Overhead aircraft had established radio contact with the pilot on the ground and we were directed into the area to assist in any way we could. I studied the map coordinates and realized we would be heading west of Hanoi, near Phuc Yen Airfield, which I knew was loaded with MiG jet fighters. My heart sank. When we went "feet dry" (crossed the coast heading inland), I thought I'd be mighty lucky to ever cross that coast again.

The downed pilot's location was in a mountainous jungle area. The USAF planes had to leave the area due to low fuel, and Ed and I with our call signs, Canasta One and Two, assumed the entire RESCAP role. After locating the pilot's position, we withdrew to the west to avoid attracting attention to the pilot and to avoid artillery fire. We flew 40 miles to the west and returned periodically to reassure the downed Air Force pilot that we knew where he was and we were not abandoning him. From overhead, we could easily see Hanoi and Phuc Yen Airfield with North Vietnamese MiGs taxiing. If they decided to launch, we could easily be sitting ducks for their air-to-air missiles.

I had calculated the fuel needed to get back to the ship as well as the fuel I would need just to get back to the coast. We had no air-to-air refueling capability. Ed and I had decided that if we were in the midst of helping the pilot get out of the jungle and the effort was looking successful, we would stay until we could only make "feet wet" (cross the coast outbound). I was willing to ditch in the Tonkin

Gulf but not ditch or bailout over North Vietnam.

Finally, in late afternoon, we got a call on the radio that the rescue helicopter was on the way. We were given a rendezvous point and escorted the chopper to the downed pilot. I was impressed with the size of the helicopter—the largest I had ever seen. Ed and I were orbiting overhead, watching for ground-based attacks directed at the helicopter or the downed pilot. Ed and I made a couple of strafing runs to try to keep the enemy's heads down while the pickup was completed. After recovery of the pilot, the helicopter lifted off and we all departed the area. We led the chopper back to the Mekong River, from whence he could find his way home.

By that time it was getting dark and I was critically low on fuel. As we crossed the coast we called our ship, the *Midway*, and told them we were inbound. We were told they had secured flight operations for the day and we should try to land at Da Nang Air Base. So much for "Welcome home, we'll keep the light on for you." They were surprised to find out we were still alive and airborne. When we got within radio range of Da Nang, we reported our low fuel state and requested a straight-in approach. I touched down at 9:45 p.m., after 9.7 hours in the air. I had less than 315 pounds of fuel in my tanks. Ed landed soon after I did. After securing the aircraft, we were off to the DOOM club for drinks and a steak. We spent the night in Da Nang and returned to the *Midway* the next afternoon.

I left the Navy in 1968, but in the back of my mind I always wondered who was rescued on July 27, 1965. In October 1993, upon returning home from dinner my daughter said, "Daddy, a man called for you tonight. He asked me where you were on July 27, 1965."

Tears came to my eyes. There were only two people other than me to whom that day meant anything special, and I had just seen Ed Greathouse the weekend before. Later, that man called again and introduced himself as Frank Tullo, the pilot we helped rescue. Frank told me how he had spent almost 30 years trying to find Canasta Flight to thank them for what they had done during his recovery.

In 1995, 30 years after the event, a reunion brought together Ed, Frank, myself, and George Martin, the helicopter pilot who had chosen his call sign as "Jolly Green" on that day so long ago. This group reconvened for a 40th anniversary on July 27, 2005.

I think I speak for Ed, and know I can say for myself, that playing a part in Frank's rescue was the single most gratifying thing that I did during two combat cruises to Vietnam.

Rescue

by
George Martin, Captain
United States Air Force

A few weeks prior to the first-ever helicopter rescue of a downed pilot deep in North Vietnam, Capt. George Martin was flying cargo support at Eglin Air Force Base in Florida. Pilots in Southeast Asia were facing the increased risk of being shot down, and therefore, the United States Air Force began training crews of the large CH-3C cargo helicopters in rescue operations. The training was to take several months but due to the urgency of the situation, two CH-3s and their crews were dispatched from Eglin to Southeast Asia. George Martin, at age 40, was deemed too old to undergo the extended training and tour of duty and was therefore sent on a 120-day assignment as commander of one of the deployed CH-3s. Martin noted, "I found out on Friday afternoon and was TDY to the Vietnam War by Sunday evening."

I was proceeding north from Nakhon Phnom Air Base, Thailand, to Lima Site 36, a secret CIA base in Laos, to assume alert status for possible rescue and recovery operations of pilots that might be shot down during air operations over North Vietnam or Laos. Adverse weather was making the trip very difficult. I joined up with two HH-43 choppers from Udorn, Thailand, and we were able to land at another secret base, Lima Site 98. While I was trying to get more information on the weather, I was alerted there was a downed pilot and urged to scramble immediately. As my crew and I embarked Site 98 en route to Site 36, we were informed that as many as four F-105s were down and we were queried as to how many trips we could make between Site 36 and the target area on one fuel load. I informed control that I needed to land at Site 36 to offload unnecessary equipment and personnel before proceeding. If I was too heavy and had to pick up more than one pilot, I would not be able to hover, and then all I could do was fly around and wave at the pilot on the ground.

As I touched down at Site 36, about 120 miles from Hanoi, my number two engine flamed out as a result of a deceleration stall, and an overtemp of 900 degrees was encountered for four or five seconds. I decided to attempt a restart after the engine cooled down, and if I could develop power, I would proceed with the mission. Everybody was pretty apprehensive. I told the crew, "We're his (the downed pilot) only hope. If the engine will start again after cool-down, we'll go." I chose as our call-sign "Jolly Green".

I reduced my crew to four personnel, engines were restarted successfully, and we departed Site 36 with 3,800 pounds of fuel. Time to target was approximately one hour and twenty minutes. Because I had no maps of the area, I was met at the Mekong River and escorted by SA-1 aircraft to within fifty miles of the target.

As I approached the target, my escort, Canasta Flight from Attack Squadron 25, USS *Midway* and I descended from 10,000 feet over the Black River and flew together at 2,000 feet to the target at 130 knots, which took about fifteen minutes. Approximately five minutes out from the target, two F-105s arrived and provided additional cover.

Contact was made with the single downed pilot exactly where Canasta Lead had directed me. He was on a steep, 45-degree, wooded slope. I established a hover eighty feet over his position and lowered the hoist. Quick engagement occurred and the pilot was pulled up ten feet when the hoist failed. All attempts to operate the hoist were ineffective. The crew chief and the paramedic attempted to pull the pilot up manually, but this also failed. I sent the co-pilot back to help, but all three could not raise him and the rope began to fray. By this time, I had been hovering for over fifteen minutes and the fire warning light on my suspect number two engine came on. The intimidating light came on twice more, and I decided to move-off my stationary position to gain airflow and cool the engine. The pilot was hanging on the rope approximately sixty feet beneath the helicopter as I commenced a slow, 360-degree climbing turn at 30 knots.

I spotted a rice paddy northwest of my position, and I dog-legged west a half-mile and then north a half-mile. We deposited the dangling pilot in the paddy and landed for pickup. As soon as our passenger was on board, I made an immediate departure, first to the west, then to the south. Approximately a half-mile after departing the landing site we encountered ground fire. It was an automatic weapon and we heard about ten shots in rapid succession. I turned southwest to the Black River and climbed to 10,000 feet, while the A-1s flew alongside until they had to leave due to a low fuel situation.

It was dark at Site 36 and the location was difficult to find, but with the help of two Air America (CIA) aircraft and flares on the runway, we made a safe landing with only 705 pounds of fuel remaining. My aircraft sustained three hits from small arms fire, resulting in minor damage. One bullet had passed through the hull right between our two non-self-sealing fuel tanks.

It had been an exciting day for a rescue helicopter and its crew. Fortunately, we all lived to tell about it. We just did our job.

The rescue of Frank Tullo was the first, (and furthest north at the time) of 1,490 recoveries made by the CH-3 "Jolly Green Giant" and its upgraded successors, the HH-3C and HH-53, in Southeast Asia. The call-sign, "Jolly Green" chosen by Capt. George Martin on July 27, 1965, lives on in the archives of rescue operations to this day, as do the names of Martin and his crew: Co-Pilot Orville N. Kreese; Crew Chief Curtis W. Pert; Paramedic Gordon C. Thayer.

George Martin - Jolly Green, and Frank Tullo - Dogwood 2, with Rescue Helicopter July 27, 1965

Dogwood 2 says "Thanks" to Jolly Green at Site 36 after the rescue, July 27, 1965

Frank Tullo and George Martin at Site 36, with other crew members July 27, 1965

Return to Base

by
Lowell Peterson, Captain
Flight Surgeon, 12th Tactical Fighter Squadron

Meanwhile, Frank Tullo, following a successful heroic rescue effort, had been flown to a Hmong village on a hilltop in Laos that was also a base camp for CIA operatives. Elated to be alive and not a POW, he proceeded to get rip-roaring drunk. The next day he was flown to Vientiane, the Capitol of Laos, which at that time had not fallen to the communist Pathet Lao. Gen. Hunter Harris, PACAF (Pacific Air Force) commander, arrived at Vientiane for an inspection visit. When he was told of Frank Tullo's downing and rescue, he offered to deliver him back to Korat in his personal Boeing 707. We, at Korat, knew General Harris would be arriving but had no idea he would have a guest with him. All of us were encouraged to be at the flightline in formation to greet the general and stand for inspection.

I will never forget the scene. The beautiful, spotless 707, painted totally white with Air Force blue trim, taxied right up in front of Base Ops. The American flag was painted on its tail. Just forward of the door, the Air Force emblem was emblazoned on its side next to four silver stars denoting the rank of General Harris. In large blue letters on the side of the fuselage it said, UNITED STATES OF AMERICA. After what we had been through in the past twenty-four hours, the sight of that impressive plane was a pep talk without words. At that moment, everyone felt a pride in their country that had been so seriously damaged a day earlier.

Then came the biggest thrill of all! The door of the Boeing 707 opened and the stairs were pushed up to the plane and secured. The red carpet was rolled out below the stairs and we were at parade-rest waiting for General Harris to disembark. Instead, Frank Tullo appeared in the door in his flight suit, with a bandage on his forehead over his left eye, flashing a wide-toothy smile and giving a wave like only Frank could do. Well, that was the end of the formation. Everyone broke ranks and ran to the plane, surrounding Frank as he descended the stairs—cheers, laughter, tears, and cries of "shit-hot!" echoing in the air.

General Harris followed Frank down the stairs, raised his hands for quiet and said, "I'm sure you wanted this guy back, and I was happy to accommodate him and be of help."

We all escorted Frank off to the briefing rooms to gather around and have him tell the story of what the past twenty-four hours had been like.

After Frank had his time with his peers, I cornered him and said we should go over to the dispensary so I could give him the once-over and make an official report on his condition. Hoz (Bill Hosmer) and Sox (Ralph Bowersox) accompanied Frank to my medical facility. On the way over, I told him, "Christ, Frank, you smell like a goat!"

Recently, Frank pointed out to me that Tom Clancy said, in his book, *Every Man a Tiger* that he had vomited on his flight suit. "I didn't, did I?" he asked me.

I reassured him that what I smelled was 24-hours of sweat and jungle grime.

At the dispensary, I examined him carefully and repaired the laceration on his forehead. When I finished, I told Hoz and Sox to take Frank over to the Officers Club and that if he had to buy a drink, I would be very disappointed in them.

I made a full medical report and figured Frank deserved the Purple Heart for what he had been through, even though his injuries were not severe. I wrote it up and submitted my report, with an unofficial recommendation for the medal. Well, all hell broke loose. I apparently did not submit it through the appropriate channels, and I was informed I had overstepped my bounds.

Frank did receive the Purple Heart and recently thanked me, saying, "I got many medals during that year, but the one I am most proud of is the one you spoke of. That was a hell of a day!"

I was moved by his gratitude, but also saddened by something else he told me.

"I was so bitter after I left the service," he said. "I was so mad; I couldn't even think or read anything about Vietnam. The lives of intelligent, hard-working young men were just being thrown away!"

Now it is for history to judge.

Takhli Debriefing

by
Paul Craw, Captain
563rd Tactical Fighter Squadron

After the mission, Brig. Gen. George Simler and Colonel Hawkins, the base commander at Takhli, were there to debrief all the flight leaders. I was asked, "What did you think of the mission?"

My response was, "I thought it was pretty fucking stupid! First, we draw 30-mile rings around both of those SAM construction sites because Mr. McNamara is afraid someone might hurt a Russian if we interfered with the site construction; and then based on a single incident, he sends 48 airplanes into a flak trap when two planes could have done the job yesterday or the day before instead of standing down."

I went on to tell General Simler, "McNamara had no idea how expensive that was going to be in the loss of men and machines."

Abruptly, my debriefing came to an end with General Simler opening the door and saying, "Next."

Gary Barnhill, a F-105 pilot, recently noted that at some point, the restriction against attacking SAMs was put back on, because U.S. planes were not allowed to touch them during September 1965. The indecision at the Pentagon on how to fight the war seemingly would never end.

It came as no surprise to me that a mission to restrike the ammunition factory was forthcoming. On August 2, 1965, the ammunition factory itself became the target with no threat of court-martial. Since the target was now reported to be heavily defended by SAM missiles, in contrast to our first trip there, two B-66 electronic surveillance aircraft were in the area to warn us of impending launch by using the code words, "The bluebells are singing."

My plan was to approach the target at 18,000 feet and roll in with all eight aircraft in a relatively tight formation. Approximately three minutes from target, the B-66s gave us the bluebells call over the radio. We pressed on and I rolled in at a steep 70-degree dive angle. (The established guidelines were to go in slower, lower, and at a shallower dive angle.) As we approached at supersonic speed the onboard computers arrived at a target solution and the bombs were released at 14,000 feet. I rolled to the left and bottomed out at about 9,000 feet. As I observed the bombs exploding, the ground suddenly disappeared below me as a result of a tremendous amount of flak exploding and dirtying the sky between 3,000 and 8,000 feet where we were expected to be. I did a 360-degree turn over the target to get my flight members joined up to head for home. We proceeded outbound well north of Yen Bai to avoid the flak along the Red River.

Our bomb damage assessment (BDA) was the most beautiful blast one could realize—we had completely destroyed the ammunition factory. What had been a court-martial crime less than one week previously was now a huge military success. I'm sure the post-strike report would have looked a whole lot different if we had followed guidelines and gone in at 5,000 feet, a 45-degree dive angle, and at 500 knots. We also would have suffered casualties of pilots and aircraft. Fortunately, no one rebuked me for my tactics or threatened me with any reprimand for trying to stay alive and successfully complete my mission.

Post-Strike Evaluation

by
Bill Hosmer, Major
Commander, Lima Flight, 12th Tactical Fighter Squadron

The day after the July 27, 1965, operation, when six Thuds (F-105s) and one EB-66 electronics surveillance aircraft were destroyed, Brig. Gen. George Simler debriefed every flight leader from both bases at Korat and Takhli, Thailand. General Simler, a well-respected leader and former commander of our 18th Tactical Fighter Wing (TFW), was very good at delving into the minds of fighter pilots to obtain insights that might improve mission results.

When he asked me for my opinion, I simply stated, "Sir, that was the dumbest operation I have ever seen or read about."

He asked me why.

I told him my opinion of what was wrong with the mission, including the number of planes, the routes, the timing, the weaponry, and the decision to go in the first place.

He responded, "Okay, you get a representative from each of the four squadrons together, and decide what means should be used to attack the SAMs (surface-to-air missiles). I want a recommendation two days from now. Also, Hoz, you'll be leading the next go."

I answered, "Yes, Sir, General."

The four of us (two from Takhli and two from Korat) got together at Korat, and spent a long day-and-a-half pouring over details, strategy, and personal experiences trying to find a way to avoid further fiascos like that of July 27. We developed a consensus of short-term tactics and weaponry options that would give the decision makers some flexibility in building a frag (mission order). We also agreed that the long-term solution was to train special air crews and outfit special airplanes with sophisticated antimissile avionics and weaponry designed to handle the ever-increasing threat posed by the SA-2 SAM. These pilots and planes would be dedicated entirely to the anti-SAM mission.

Two days later the four of us presented our recommendations to General

Simler. The general said he agreed with the long-term solution, but for the short-range, he indicted that our preference for small flights with a maximum of four airplanes wouldn't be acceptable to the headquarter's staff in Saigon. "They wish to see a lot of craters around target sites in the BDA (bomb drop area)."

This ludicrous thinking for the purpose of pleasing Secretary McNamara, the Pentagon, and the press was being carried out at the expense of great losses of pilots and planes. It was like doing body counts of casualties—ours versus theirs—to prove to the President and the public that we were winning the war.

I flew four more anti-SAM missions, one of which was a twelve-shipper. By the time we got to the site, the SAMs had been relocated, but the antiaircraft guns were still there. We put our ordnance on the location anyway, but the lesson learned was that these sites were quite mobile. We had a pre-strike photo taken by an F-101 pilot earlier in the day, showing SAMs at the site, but by the time we responded, they had moved. The good news was that this time we achieved tactical surprise at low level, and had zero losses. That was such a relief because the SAMs were deployed very close to Hanoi with its heavy antiaircraft and MiG defenses, and I was fearful this might be a repeat of that awful day at the end of July.

Within a year the Air Force did organize and deploy Wild Weasel F-100s (two-seater fighter aircraft with a pilot and an electronic countermeasure weapons officer) to deal with the SAM threat. This force was led by Gary Willard. Later the smaller, slower F-100s were replaced by larger, faster, two-seater F105Gs with improved radar detection and electronic countermeasure capabilities. The tremendous record they achieved is a hallmark, unmatched in the annals of heroism and strike-force protection. Certainly the four of us did not originate the idea of the Wild Weasel, but we uttered the first words on the subject that I know of. I have always felt a kinship to the Weasels because what we learned on July 27, 1965, brought us up a very steep learning curve in a hurry. If we hadn't heeded the lesson, we would have been destined to relive the experience over and over again.

IV
CAPTIVITY AND TORTURE

If I could ever forgive ... the inhumane living conditions and physical torture ... It will be even more difficult to find forgiveness for the mental deprivation they forced on us ... The mental anxieties caused by 6$^1/_2$ years with nothing to occupy the mind controls my deepest hatred for these people. Time has healed the physical pain ...

Lt. Fred Flom
354th TFS, 355 TFW
POW August 1966 - March 1973

Wes Schierman and his "Silver Bird"

A Bad Day at Son La

by
Wes Schierman, Captain
67th Tactical Fighter Squadron

On August 27, 1965, I was assigned to plan and lead a mission on the following day to bomb a military barracks area near Son La, North Vietnam, one hundred miles west of Hanoi. Four aircraft, each carrying eight 500-pound MK-82 "snake-eye" bombs, were assigned to the mission. These bombs had four large metal fins that popped out when released. The fins were designed to slow the bomb so they could be delivered at low altitude and explode at the drop-point without damage to the aircraft. This mission would be the first time these bombs would be dropped from a F-105 in combat.

When I studied all of the test data available from the Weapons Test Center at Nellis Air Force Base, I found that no one had ever dropped more than four snake-eye bombs successfully off the centerline station under the fuselage of the F-105. If more were loaded and armed, the bombs would either run into each other and explode prematurely, or the fins would fail. In either case, the aircraft was damaged. Because it had been determined that four could be dropped without malfunction, I went to the Wing Operations Officer, Paul Kunichika, and requested he advise Second Air Division in Saigon that there was no way I would carry six of these bombs centerline and two on the outboard stations. But, if it was really an important target, I would carry four. I also wanted Sidewinder air-to-air missiles on the outboard wing stations in place of two of the bombs because the target was near a MiG air base. I told Major Kunichika I thought the mission was a bad idea.

At Wing Operations the next morning, Paul advised me Saigon had agreed. We had a 0900 take-off time for a 1000 time on target (TOT). Following weather and intelligence briefings, I briefed my pilots in "blue flight"—each of the flights making up the 67th Squadron was designated by color—on the mission details. I was advised I would be flying a two-seat F-105F because my F-105D had not passed its preflight checks. I would be designated with the call sign as Elm Lead.

Our startup, taxi, and takeoff were right on time. We rendezvoused with the tanker and completed our refueling. It all went like clockwork. We proceeded from the refueling point north over the Mekong River, making a Doppler navigational update over the TACAN station near Sam Neua (New-E) in northern Laos. We descended down to low-level as we crossed the border into North Vietnam from Laos, using the ground-mapping radar and Doppler to navigate to our turning point at Highway 6, just west of Nasan Airfield. As I turned on course for the target, I was flying 400 feet above ground level (AGL) at 420 knots, heading northwest, parallel to the highway. I could not see anything resembling a barrack's area and realized the coordinates we had been given were wrong. Finally, I spotted the target about one mile south of the highway instead of north of the highway, as our coordinates had indicated. Since I was already past the target, I pointed it out to my second element leader and cleared him to drop first, heading southeast, while I brought my flight around to make our bombing pass. After we dropped our bombs, I turned around enough to see the target, but I could not tell how much damage was done.

We had also been ordered to continue reconnaissance for targets along the road to Dien Bien Phu, so I instructed my flight to do a 180° turn for a strafing pass back to the west. I made a left turn, rolled in, and fired a burst from my gun at the barracks. After one second, the gun stopped firing in spite of the fact that I still had the trigger depressed. I was thinking, "That's odd," when I heard and felt a loud clunk on the left side of the aircraft, followed almost immediately by a very loud explosion in the aft section of the airplane. Then, the engine stopped. (I later concluded my gun had malfunctioned, ejecting metal pieces into the air intake, causing the engine to explode.)

I called the other pilots in the flight and said, "Elm Lead is hit; I have to get out!" I knew I did not have enough altitude to get out of the valley, so I continued straight ahead toward a small hill, a couple of miles away.

About that time my number four man called, "Lead, you've got fire coming out of the back!"

My airspeed was dropping rapidly as I approached the hill so I said, "I'm getting out!" I raised the handgrips of the ejection seat with my left hand, which blew off the canopy. My airspeed dropped below 220 knots. I checked the position of my body in the seat and squeezed the trigger. As the seat fired out of the aircraft, I was aware of two sensations: a sharp pain in my lower back and an extreme wind blast hitting me in the face. Within seconds, the seat left me and I felt the soft opening shock of the parachute. Just when I thought all was well, I felt a very heavy impact on the left side of my body. I looked up and saw the ejection seat tangled in the risers of my chute. I was only around 1,000 feet above the ground and did not have time to free the seat from the risers, so I held it away with my arms and prepared for landing. I hit the ground pretty hard, which knocked the wind out of me, but after a short time I recovered and was relieved to find I had suffered no major injuries.

I landed near the top of the small hill and quickly concealed my parachute, helmet, ejection seat, and survival kit as best I could. I discovered I had received a very deep cut in my left wrist, which was bleeding profusely, so I tied a compress bandage on it as tightly as I could. I contacted my wingmen and they advised me the rescue helicopter was on its way and that they would "cap" me as long as their fuel would allow. The city of Son La was to my right, and there was a small village to my left. I concluded that any direction I went, I would run into searchers looking for me, so I elected to stay on top of the hill. My flight called and advised me they would have to depart due to low fuel, but that Colonel Risner's flight was diverting to come in and take the cap.

About five minutes later, I heard voices coming up the hill from the south and from the east. I burrowed down into the thickest cover I could find. When the Vietnamese soldiers arrived, I saw there was a platoon of regular infantry with automatic weapons and grenade launchers. They found my chute, then swept up the hill past my position, but failing to find me, returned to the chute and repeated the process again. About the fourth time through, one of them almost stepped on me and I was discovered. I turned my beeper homing radio on as they dragged me out of the brush. They took my boots and stripped my gear off of me just as the RC-54 (Rescue Coordinator Aircraft) appeared overhead, with the helicopter close behind. So close; so close! That had to be the lowest point in my life. The Vietnamese, very concerned about the aircraft overhead, tied my arms behind me, looped the rope around my neck, and started running me down the hill through the brush, slipping and falling until we were concealed under the jungle canopy.

Colonel Risner's flight located some North Vietnamese gun positions that were firing at them, and they began making strafing passes with their guns and also were firing their bullpup missiles at the targets. It was an awesome sound! The Vietnamese soon realized my beeper was transmitting and made me turn it off.

I was kept in a small cave with a locked gate across the entrance, under guard, for the next three days and nights. I was then transported to Hanoi under heavy guard. We would stay in truck parks under heavy tree cover during the day to avoid airstrikes. I only received about a pint of water per day and was very thirsty.

I arrived in Hanoi at Hoa Lo Prison (The Hanoi Hilton) on the morning of 3 September 1965. The Vietnamese could kill me any time they chose, but I told myself that fear would not cause me to compromise my principles. I would follow the Code of Conduct to the best of my ability. I had been taught these guidelines at Stead Air Force Base survival school: Be military; Don't discuss or argue politics; Don't ask for anything; Follow the Code of Conduct.

As the large, iron gate at the entrance to Hoa Lo Prison slammed shut behind me, I began a new kind of war. It was a war of wills—theirs against mine, and mine against theirs. And I made up my mind that I would rather not return home than dishonor myself, my family, or my country.

Heartbreak Hotel—Cell Number 1
The Nightmare Begins

by
Wes Schierman, Captain
67ᵗʰ Tactical Fighter Squadron

I was placed in a solitary room in the area the prisoners had named "New Guy Village". Within hours, I was escorted to an initial interrogation—the first of many, which occurred day and night for the next ten days. I gave only my name, rank, serial number, and date of birth as required by the Geneva Convention. The Vietnamese stated that there was no declared war, that I was a criminal in their country, and that I would be tortured or killed if I did not answer their questions. There were many threats and they slapped me around, but I refused to tell them anything else. The laceration on my wrist became infected and the Vietnamese offered me medical attention if I would answer their questions. I refused. At the end of the ten days I was given my last chance to answer or be killed. I politely refused.

Having called their bluff, I was moved into a small cellblock in a building we called Heartbreak Hotel. There was a center corridor with four cells on each side. I was placed in cell number 1, right across the hall from cell number 8, which served as a cold water bathing area and also as the place our waste buckets were emptied.

Shortly after the guard left, I heard a voice softly calling from another cell, "Hey, new guy, what's your name?"

I got down on the floor, and talking under the door, I answered, "This is Air Force Captain Wes Schierman."

The voice replied, "Hi, Wes, this is Percy."

I couldn't believe it! Bob Purcell from the 12ᵗʰ Squadron shot down in July 1965, was presumed killed-in-action. I had attended his memorial service. Percy gave me the names of all the others in the cellblock, including "Smitty" Harris, the first man from our 67ᵗʰ Squadron to be captured on April 4, 1965. Ron Byrne, a flight commander from my squadron, was shot down the day after I was, but closer to Hanoi, so he beat me there. I was able to give Smitty information about his son who was born six weeks after he was captured.

I was told of a hidden mailbox behind a loose brick in the shower area where notes could be exchanged. I received a copy of the tap code and Morse code, which were to become our lifeline, and often our only means of communication, for many years. I was also given a list of the known POW names to memorize, and found that I was number 23. In later years, I had amassed a list of 368 names, which I reviewed in my head on a daily basis.

I received a thin straw mat, one set of long clothes, one set of short clothes, a pair of rubber tire sandals, a blanket, a toothbrush to last six months, a tube of toothpaste to last three months, a small water pitcher, a cup, and a spoon. Later, I received a second blanket and a sweatshirt, which were blessings during the cold, damp winters.

When I was caught communicating, I was placed in stocks built into the foot of the concrete beds. I could only sit or lie on my back, but could not turn over or use the waste bucket. I was absolutely miserable, but I managed to get through the first twenty-four hours and decided to take it one day at a time. I was released on the morning of the fourth day. Another prisoner, Nels Tanner, went one hundred twenty-eight consecutive days locked in the stocks.

On September 17, 1965, a new POW was brought in. In response to the "new guy" question, the reply came back, "This is Col. Robinson Risner, who's in charge here?"

We knew right away who was going to be in charge. Colonel Risner, my squadron commander, a Korean War ace, was captured after his second shoot-down in six months. Maj. Ray Merritt had provided rescue cover (RESCAP) for Colonel Risner and had been shot down himself. We now had five men from the same squadron in our tiny cellblock. In late September we were moved to a new camp in Hanoi, which we called The Zoo. Living conditions deteriorated as did our diet, which consisted of a small plate of rice, a cup of thin soup, a couple of bites of pig fat, or some kind of vegetable or root, and very little water.

As the North Vietnamese became more and more frustrated in their efforts to acquire information and cooperation from the POWs, they became more threatening. In October I underwent interrogations, or quizzes as we called them, lived alone in a dark room full of mosquitoes, and was hungry and thirsty twenty-four hours a day. It was very demoralizing. Were it not for the ability to communicate, I can't imagine how we would have coped. I used Morse code to talk with the man next door, Ed Davis. He was my only contact for two months. I actually reached the point where I was dreaming in Morse code.

A note with resistance instructions from Colonel Risner and a map of the Zoo were discovered by the Vietnamese, so they moved him back to the Hilton where he was severely abused for many months. The Vietnamese then published camp regulations stating that we were not POWs but war criminals, and that we were to do anything they said, or we would be punished.

Thus began the systematic torture that would last for the next four and one-half years. This consisted of moving the subject to an isolation room where he would be placed in tight handcuffs, with his arms twisted up behind his back. He would then be forced to sit on a low stool, twenty-four hours a day, with no food, very little water, and no sleep. If caught off the stool or asleep, the guards would come in and beat him with their rifle butts, bamboo poles, feet, and fists. After a few days or weeks of this, they would wrap ropes tightly around the biceps and draw the arms up further behind the back while, at the same time forcing the head down between the legs. The rope might then be passed over the shoulders down to leg irons, pulling the arms higher until the shoulders dislocated. Due to the compression of the chest, breathing was greatly restricted, and suffocation could occur. Circulation was cut off in the arms by the ropes, making them feel like they had been thrust into boiling water. They tortured us to coerce us to make good treatment statements, propaganda statements and, the one we feared most of all, war crimes confessions. The Vietnamese became very proficient at obtaining what they wanted and all the prisoners found that they had a breaking point. The guilt and remorse of being broken was devastating, but because we could communicate, we found we were not alone in our devastation. We were just human.

In early December 1965, I was moved to a camp in the hills about thirty-five miles west of Hanoi, which we named The Briarpatch. The two main interrogators at the Briarpatch were "Frenchy" and "Bug". We nicknamed all of the interrogators, being as derogatory as we could. Frenchy could be quite charming and intelligent, but he could also, when angered, turn into a raving, frothing at the mouth, madman. Bug had eyes that stared off in different directions and hair that stood straight up like a caterpillar's. He was more controlled, but sneering, sinister, and vicious. During my quizzes, I used every stalling technique I could think of to drag things out.

On January 15, 1966, I was placed in handcuffs in my cell and on February 3rd I was put on half rations. On February 21st, I was put in the ropes for the first time. I managed to last about twenty-four hours before I concluded that I could stand no more pain and would have to agree to answer their questions. Over the next year, I would be put in the ropes or tight cuffs five more times.

On July 6, 1966, sixteen of us from the Briarpatch were blindfolded, handcuffed in pairs, and loaded into trucks and moved to Hanoi Stadium. That evening, we, along with thirty-six others from the Hilton, were handcuffed together in pairs and paraded through the streets of Hanoi where the Vietnamese people were incited to show their hatred. We were pelted with rocks, sticks, and bottles. The parade turned into a mob scene. Back in the stadium, we collapsed on the ground, battered and bloody.

One of the newer POWs, Cole Black, asked, "Do you guys do this very often?"

Chuck Boyd replied, "No, only on Saturdays."

It was the first laugh we had had in a longtime. Following the march, I was given a roommate, Ron Storz.

By December 1966, many of the POWs had pain and stiffness in their hands and feet accompanied by severe swelling. It was determined that most of us had beriberi, caused by a vitamin deficiency. On February 2, 1967, the Briarpatch was closed and we were moved back to Hanoi where we were given a small half-loaf of French bread instead of rice, and the beriberi eventually subsided. Occasionally, I would get a banana, which I dutifully peeled and ate. The first time, I threw the peeling away. But later I reasoned that there had to be some nutrition in the peel. From then on, I ate the banana, peeling and all. We all had dysentery from our watery rice diet, but when I ate the banana peel, my diarrhea improved or went away, for whatever reason. I was also given an occasional cigarette, but never more than three a day. I did not smoke, so I saved the paper to write notes on, and chewed the tobacco, swallowing it rather than spitting it out. I found that I rather liked the high the nicotine gave me, and always looked forward to the next one. An added benefit was that the tobacco juice flushed the pinworms and two large tapeworms from my system.

When we became severely ill, or had a fever, the Vietnamese medic would sometimes come with a whole handful of pills and force us to take them. It was shotgun therapy for whatever ailed us. Some POWs died in prison due to malnutrition or the aftereffects of the beatings, infections, or improperly treated medical conditions.

When we were moved back to the Hanoi Hilton, we established contact with Navy Comdr. James Stockdale, who was senior ranking officer because Colonel Risner was still in isolation. There was a communication purge going on as the Vietnamese tried to suppress all resistance. Commander Stockdale and many other leaders were severely tortured. Eventually, my name came up and I, too, was tortured for three days in a row. Following this torture my roommate, Ron Storz and many others, were moved to a bad-guy camp we called Alcatraz. Due to constant illness and abuse, Ron died there in April of 1970.

I also became very ill and very weak, and my weight dropped to less than one hundred pounds. Eventually, I received the shotgun antibiotic treatment and recovered. I finally concluded that to punish oneself by resisting was self-defeating and that it was better to endure the beatings than to go without sleep or food while opposing their demands.

At Son Tay, because of my defiance, I was tortured on the stool for about two weeks. My legs were pulled back and the leg irons were passed through the rungs of the stool so that the iron bar supported the weight of my legs on my shinbones. It was extremely painful. I could not walk and had to crawl to the door to pick up my food when I was released for fifteen minutes. I was released and given a reprieve only after I agreed to write an apology to the camp commander.

In September of 1969, Ho Chi Minh died and the North Vietnamese announced a policy change. They said they were improving the conditions and we would no longer be needed for propaganda. Their friends in America, such as Jane Fonda, Ramsey Clark, and Wayne Morse were helping them now. At Christmas of 1969, I received a package from my family. I had not been allowed to write or receive any mail prior to this time.

An aerial view of the Hanoi Hilton
Photo courtesy of www.wikipedia.com

Hope for Freedom Day

by
Wes Schierman, Captain
67th Tactical Fighter Squadron

On July 14, 1970, we were moved from Son Tay to a new camp about ten miles closer to Hanoi, which we named Camp Faith. The conditions and treatment were significantly better than at Son Tay. We began to receive condensed milk and canned meat from the Soviet Union and China. In September 1970, I was allowed to send and receive a seven-line form letter to and from my family for the first time.

At about 2 a.m. on the morning of November 21, 1970, we awoke to the sound of gunfire and SAM missiles being fired from just outside our camp. We could see flares being dropped to the West. Our guards were on full alert, carrying gas masks and hand grenades. They appeared very agitated. Two days later, almost all of the POWs in North Vietnam were moved back to the Hanoi Hilton complex, into larger fifty-man rooms, in an area we named Camp Unity. We found out that there had been some kind of commando raid and within a week we heard Hanoi Hannah on the Voice of Vietnam complaining about the U.S. invasion of North Vietnam. We guessed that it had been a raid on a POW camp. We found out it was Son Tay. The raid was ordered by the new Secretary of Defense for President Nixon, Melvin Laird. Intelligence had indicated the presence of humans within the camp, but, unfortunately, we had been moved. The North Vietnamese soldiers who had moved in after our departure were the only remaining occupants and were killed by the raiders. One could say the mission was a failure—still, just knowing that we had not been forgotten was a great boost to our morale.

Because we were in larger rooms in greater numbers, we were able to organize our activities, come up with entertainment, and hold educational classes. Under the direction of Colonel Risner, Commander Stockdale, and Colonel Flynn, the new senior ranking officer (SRO), the 4th Allied POW Wing was formed, with a commander, executive officer, and wing staff. Perhaps because the Vietnamese recognized our senior officers could control us better than they could, they allowed us some freedom.

We always tried to have church services on Sunday. Each room had a choir, but we were not allowed to congregate in large groups. In March of 1971, we began a combined church service against their rules, and, as the guards arrived to take away Colonel Risner and several others who were leading the service, Bud Day (a medal of honor recipient), began to sing the "Star Spangled Banner". Everyone joined in, and soon, the whole group of American POWs were singing. We sang "God Bless America" and other patriotic songs before the riot squad arrived with fixed bayonets and escorted many men to Heartbreak Hotel, where they lived under poor conditions, for several months. I was one of those moved to Heartbreak and the conditions were miserable. I decided to protest our conditions by shaving my head in a Mohawk-style haircut. That earned me a quiz by the "Bug". Eventually, the Vietnamese allowed a full church service, but told us not to sing too loud.

In March of 1972, President Nixon ordered the resumption of bombing of North Vietnam and in mid-May, 209 POWs were moved from Camp Unity, 200 miles north to Cao Bang near the Chinese border. We named this camp, Dogpatch. On the first night, one of my cellmates entered our room with a dim oil lamp and detected movement. A guard was summoned with a flashlight and discovered a five-foot Cobra, which the guards killed.

In December 1972, we learned of the B-52 bombings of Hanoi during Operation Linebacker. This operation led to the negotiated settlement and our release. Unfortunately, some POWs died before they could be repatriated. Many were sent home seriously wounded and required amputations and lengthy hospitalizations.

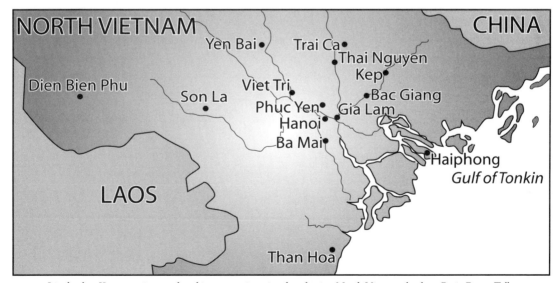

Linebacker II was an intense bombing campaign aimed at forcing North Vietnam back to Paris Peace Talks

On the evening of February 11, 1973, a group of us were issued a new set of clothes and the next morning were taken to Gia Lam airport, crossing the Red River on a pontoon bridge, because the Doumer Bridge had been destroyed. We were met by a U.S. Air Force colonel and escorted to a C-141. When we got airborne and the gear came up, a tremendous celebration erupted, with everyone cheering and shouting. When the pilot announced that we were out of North Vietnam airspace, we went wild! Our dream of Freedom Day had finally come true!

Author's Note: Of the 802 Southeast Asia prisoners of war (POWs), 472 were imprisoned and tortured in North Vietnam. Included in their number were Medal of Honor recipients: USAF Col. George "Bud" Day, Navy Vice Adm. James B. Stockdale, USAF Col. Leo Thorsness, and USA M. Sgt. Jon Caviani. Four other POWs, USA Capt. Rocky Versace, USAF Capt. Lance Sijan, USA E-3 William D. Port, and USMC Donald G. Cook, received the Medal of Honor posthumously.

The C-141 Starlifter
Becomes "The Hanoi Taxi"

by Lowell Peterson, Captain
Flight Surgeon, 12th Tactical Fighter Squadron

The C-141 Starlifter arrived at Kadena Air Base in the spring of 1966 to huge fanfare. Oh, yes, there had been the birth of the F-105, the F-4C, the C-130, the secret U-2, and other cutting-edge aircraft, but this was something different. Unlike the old propeller-driven cargo planes, such as the C-124 "Old Shakey", the C-130 Hercules turboprop, and World War II leftovers like the C-47 or C-54, the C-141 Starlifter cargo-troop carrier from Lockheed was mammoth in its proportions. It had a droop-wing and high T-tail design not seen on previous transport aircraft.

In spite of its innate beauty and size, I had a certain amount of skepticism about this airplane and its capabilities. Perhaps it just seemed too big—a 168-foot-long behemoth, capable of carrying 34 tons of cargo or more than 200 soldiers, and able to fly at 500 mph above 40,000 feet. I had to wonder if it would hold together.

Previously, the USAF had developed the C-133, an airplane that could carry larger cargo loads longer distances and at faster speeds than the C-130, but it also had an eerie tendency to disappear without warning, without explanation, without an SOS call, without anything. It happened once or twice at Okinawa. An airplane took off under the cover of darkness and disappeared. It was as if the plane, crew, and cargo had been swallowed up by the night itself. Rumor suggested that the C-133s broke apart suddenly due to structural stress and shifting cargo. With the advent of the Starlifter, I couldn't help wondering if aircraft companies were building bigger and more powerful machines in a race to win government contracts without adequate concern for safety.

The C-141 flew its maiden flight at Kadena Air Force Base, and it was flawless. Col. Bill Mitchell, the Military Airlift Command (MAC) commander, and dignitaries were allowed to take a signature cruise flight. I was thrilled to be on the flight line to see it take off and land. That old World War II warrior, Col. Bill Mitchell, extolled its praises. He had taken the controls and said that it behaved like a babe-

C-141

in-arms. And, I thought, "If he loves it, I love it."

Seven years later, the C-141 Starlifter had established an impeccable record for safety and an outstanding combat transport record. And, it was chosen to be the "Hanoi Taxi," which would retrieve and ferry the freed prisoners of war from Gia Lam Airport in Hanoi, North Vietnam, to Clark Air Force Base in the Philippines. So, on February 12, 1973, the C-141 became more than a cargo plane. It was a messianic silver bird sent to liberate the men of the United States military who had given more than any rational human being should ever expect to have to give.

Colonel Larry Guarino, in his book, *A POW's Story: 2801 Days in Hanoi*, describes it this way:

> *An hour after our arrival at Gia Lam, we heard the welcome sound of approaching aircraft. Looking toward the end of the runway, we could see a beautiful silver bird just touching down—it was a type I had never seen before, a four-engine jet transport, called the C-141 Starlifter. I climbed aboard that beautiful airplane ... the pilot did a fast taxi to the end of the runway ... the bird shuddered ... then the four engines screamed at maximum power. The bird surged forward, and, in seconds, we were racing down the runway ... the bird rotated and stood on its main wheels ..., then it leapt into the air—We're FREE ... FREE ... FREE!!!!!!*

Now, the C-141 is in mothballs, retired by advancing technology, but it has left an impressive legacy. It delivered necessary cargo and troops ten thousand miles to a foreign land to defend and enhance the principles of free people everywhere, and in the end, it brought its combatants home. The "Hanoi Taxi" served its country well.

V
REQUIEM TO WAR

The truth about Vietnam that revisionist historians conveniently forget is that the United States had not lost when we withdrew in 1973. From the Tet Offensive in 1968 up to the fall of Saigon in 1975, South Vietnam never lost a major battle. The Tet Offensive itself was a victory for South Vietnam and devastated the North Vietnamese army, which lost 289,000 men in 1968 alone.

Melvin R. Laird
2005

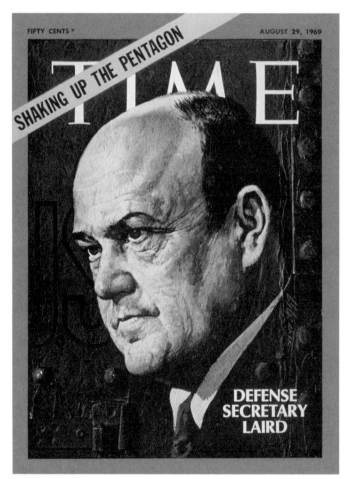

Did We Win or Lose?

by

John Morrissey, Colonel, USAF (Ret.)

In early 1968, three very important things happened. There was the TET Offensive, after which Walter Cronkite proclaimed that we had lost the war. Then, President Lyndon Johnson announced he would not run for office again. At the same time, we had the battle of Khe San, which was ballyhooed by the press and by the North Vietnamese as a major defeat for the United States. The TET Offensive and the battle of Khe San were anything but major Viet Cong and North Vietnamese victories. Our troops actually won those firefights, inflicting heavy casualties. They were not our Dien Bien Phu. The enemy had been severely and critically crippled. So what happened? Lyndon Johnson called a bombing halt, which allowed the Viet Cong and North Vietnamese to recover, regroup, and re-supply. Thereafter, nothing significant happened until Richard Nixon became President and Henry Kissinger, Secretary of State.

On the day that Saigon fell in April 1975, I was teaching the history of air warfare at the Army Command and General Staff College at Fort Leavenworth, Kansas. As I watched my student officers from Cambodia and South Vietnam, I suddenly realized that the countries they knew had ceased to exist. They were men without a country. I almost quit the Air Force that day. I could not believe my country would fight so long and then just give up.

When I visited Hanoi in 2000, I walked across the re-built Doumer Bridge. I saw the prisons. I walked the ground where the B-52 bombing strikes in Operation Linebacker II of December 1972 took place. I believe these bombings not only inflicted tremendous damage on Hanoi, but also worked on the minds of the communist leaders of North Vietnam, reducing their will to fight. At the same time, however, the will of the U.S. to continue the war had also been severely compromised. I believe all of these factors led to negotiation of the Paris Peace Accord, the U.S. withdrawal from Vietnam, and the release of our POWs.

I also went back to Korat in December 1996, almost twenty-four years to the day after Linebacker II was over. The defense attaché and the Thai Wing Commander picked up my wife and me at Siam Intercontinental Hotel in Bangkok and drove us to Korat. I stood on the flight line at Korat and watched as the last boards of our USAF operational building, Fort Apache, were being carried away. There was a beautiful F-16 squadron building and a squadron of equally good-looking F-16s, but there was only one Thai F-16 pilot and one crew chief at the squadron building.

It was 84 degrees, with a two or three knot wind and no clouds in the sky, just as it had been thirty-plus years before. It was absolutely quiet, absolutely peaceful, and I thought to myself, "What would it be like here today, had we never showed up in 1965?" In 1996, there was no longer any American air power in the Pacific west of Okinawa or south of Korea. I knew in my heart that Thailand was free and Cambodia was free, and that the efforts of the United States Air Force had helped make that possible.

CLOSURE

That our effort in Vietnam proved unwise does not make their sacrifice less noble. It endures for all to see. Let us learn from their sacrifice and, by doing so, validate and honor it.

> Robert S. McNamara
> 1995

We who came home must never forget those who could not.

> Motto: the Red River Valley
> Fighter Pilot Association
> (The River Rats)

Peace without victory is the natural ideal of the man who is too proud to fight. It is spurned by all men of lofty soul, by all men fit to call themselves fellow citizens of Washington and Lincoln, or of the warworn fighters who followed Grant and Lee."

> Theodore Roosevelt
> 1916

Doc and Frank Street join the River Rats in silent reflection at the Vietnam War Memorial Wall

*… 58,000 names carved
into the black stone,
and I suddenly saw
these men as kids,
carefully carving
their names into trees,
into school desks,
into wooden fences.
I realized that
for every name
in the granite,
there was a matching
name still carved
somewhere in America,
and their names, too,
were carved in the
hearts of their families
and in the heart
of the nation.*

Nelson DeMille
2002

Photos courtesy of wikipedia.com

VI
VIGNETTES OF AIR FORCE LIFE—1963 - 1966

Duties and Deployments

by
Bill Hosmer, Major
Commander, Lima Flight, 12th Tactical Fighter Squadron

I came to Kadena Air Force Base (AFB), Okinawa, in 1963 after completing a two-year tour as the left-wing pilot for the United States Air Force Thunderbird aerial demonstration team. Before I left the United States, I checked-out in the F-105 at Nellis Air Force Base. One of the other student pilots was James "Black Matt" Matthews. I never knew for absolute certainty why he was called "Black Matt," but I suspect it was because of his heavy head of jet-black hair, his dark bushy eyebrows, and his trimmed black mustache. We found out we were both going to the 18th Tactical Fighter Wing (TFW), and we looked forward to a long friendship. Matt was assigned to the 67th Squadron and I was assigned to the 12th Squadron at Kadena AFB.

I was assigned to an Air Task Force (ATF) flight, led by Tom Kozak. Others assigned to that flight were: Dick Doucette, Chuck Kochi, George Sasser, Jay Mitchell, J. C. Jones, and a young lieutenant, named Frank Tullo. John Neil was the squadron commander and Bill Craig was the operations officer. His assistant, Jim "White Fang" Hartney, was a miracle of diplomacy, loyalty, and lethality. Sadly, Jim was killed in the Vietnam fracas on a Thud (F-105) mission over North Vietnam. In 1964 John Neil was replaced by Bob Fair as squadron commander, Tom Kozak returned to Nellis AFB, Las Vegas, and I was designated ATF commander of Lima Flight of the 12th Squadron. When Bob Fair assumed command, things became extremely enlivened because of his impressive leadership style. His example, his expectations, and his exuberance inspired me in a big way, and being in his squadron as an ATF commander was an honor I will never forget. It was the best job, working for the best guy, I experienced in my Air Force career.

My upgrading to nuclear alert capability in the F-105 took the normal amount of time. It was complex and critical in many different ways, and horrendously grave in its implications. The odds of surviving the missions to our targets would be slim, at best.

The ATFs were gifted with deployments to various locations in the Pacific Air Force (PACAF) area, which allowed us to get away from the nuclear alert pad for an extended period of time. One of the first deployments on temporary duty assignment (TDY) was an exercise in Formosa (Taiwan), with ground forces, air exercises, and other missions of a non-nuclear nature. This was a lot of fun and a real treat. One of the social occasions with the Nationalist Chinese Air Force included a lot of toasts with rice wine, and a banquet of delicacies, including whole chickens with claws still attached to their legs, and the heads intact, eyes included. For us Americans, the salad was looking better and better.

The Chinese shuttled different pilots in and out of the room, proposed more toasts, and remained sober while they watched us get totally soused. Frank Tullo and Matt Kelch from our squadron remember that after we had finished dinner and our many, many toasts, I excused myself, turned around, grabbed a handful of napkins from the table behind ours, and as quietly as possible, vomited into the napkins, threw them over the balcony railing into the street, wiped my mouth daintily, and continued the conversation. Later that night, when we returned to our barracks, Paul Craw and I were

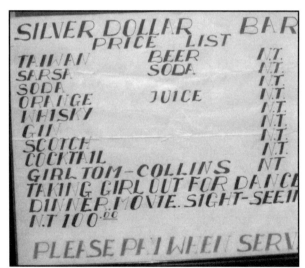

Taiwan menu in new Taiwan dollars
Photo courtesy of Matt Kelch

among the last two to use the latrine before retiring. I said, "I was sure glad I ate those chicken legs claw first because if I had not, my throat would have been torn to shreds when I threw up." Immediately, four other guys sprang out of their cots and regurgitated into the facilities.

When we got back to Kadena, a new squadron weapons officer named Bob Purcell was assigned to my flight for scheduling and administrative matters. Purcell and I shook hands and after that everything was in "full burner", and we weren't even close to the runway. I loved the guy right from the start and was so happy and fortunate to have him in Lima Flight.

Lima flight was dispatched TDY a second time to Kung Kuan Air Base, Formosa, to participate in a fly-by over Taipei on "10-10" day, commemorating 10 October 1949, when Chiang Kai-shek established the Nationalist Chinese government of

Taiwan. The weather was questionable, but, as they say, the show must go on.

The original order tasking the mission called for 180 aircraft to fly by the reviewing stand in Taipei in four-plane diamond formations, with one diamond following another, ad infinitum, for the benefit of the Generalissimo and his party. We were all under the command of a Chinese general who was leading a flight of F-86s, followed by many other types of Chinese aircraft, including F-104s. We were one of four diamonds of sixteen U.S. Air Force aircraft, followed by diamonds of equal numbers of U.S. Navy and Marine aircraft. In front of us were nine diamonds of sixteen aircraft each, representing each Nationalist Chinese Fighter Wing. I was leading our diamond, Frank Tullo was on my left wing, Bob Purcell was on my right wing, and George Sasser was in the slot.

The Chinese general said that he would maintain 300 knots, plus-or-minus 5 knots, which turned out to be a joke. In order to maintain spacing on those ahead of me, I was forced to vary power from idle and speed brakes, to full afterburner along the route to the reviewing area. We made the descent to our assigned review altitude over the ocean north of Taipei, flying between mountains on the left and right, and under a cloud cover above. I felt like I was flying through a tunnel. As our flight was about four formations from the reviewing stand, there was a huge fireball, caused by an obvious mishap just ahead. Someone yelled, "Watch out for chutes," which was followed by a plethora of radio transmissions that garbled up the airways in a bad way. My right wingman, Bob "Percy" Purcell transmitted a radio call which brought order back from mayhem. He said, "Everybody, shut up and fly formation!" The radio went quiet, everybody followed his order, and we maintained our designated headings until we passed the reviewing stand and ascended up over the clouds and returned to land at Kung Kuan. Percy's call was one of the most significant peacetime calls I ever heard. As leader of the flight, I wished I had thought of it.

When we landed and met with the Chinese pilots, they told us what had happened. The right wingman of a four-ship F-104 flight hit a radio antenna right in front of the Generalissimo. This made him fall back out of formation. After recovering, he was trying to rejoin his flight. The leader and the slot man in the formation were both looking over their shoulders, watching him rejoin, when the leader suddenly noticed his airplane was going to enter a cloud bank. He applied forward stick pressure to try to stay in the clear. The slot man was still watching the other guy over his shoulder, and collided with the lead aircraft. Both aircraft crashed in flames. Later, while having a drink with the Chinese Nationalist pilots, they said, "Good thing they died; most embarrassing to all of us."

Later, back at Kadena, we had a formal dining-in, at which we were enjoying the usual flow of alcohol and good food. Maj. Gen. A. P. Clark, the 313th Air Division commander approached me and said that he had been standing next to Generalissimo Chiang Kai-shek during the fly-by on 10-10 day. He asked me what it looked like from my perspective.

I said, "Sir, one of my flight members made a radio call which prevented a possible disaster."

He said, "I would like to meet that man."

I sent someone to get Percy away from the punch bowl. As Percy approached, I said, "General Clark, this is the man who made the call; this is Captain Purcell."

As they shook hands, Percy said to General Clark, "Yes sir, I remember you; we were classmates, and you got all the breaks."

That was the end of that conversation! I guess Percy figured (if he was capable of it at the time), that a little dig was better than receiving a decoration.

There were many peacetime events around Kadena AFB which were memorable, especially when we were not on the nuclear alert pad or preparing for operational readiness inspections (ORIs). One time Percy and I had completed our turn on the pad, and after being relieved, decided to have a few Heinekens in the Stag Bar at the club. When we left the club after dark to head through Koza City to our respective off-base housing neighborhoods on our motor scooters, it began to rain. As we headed through Koza, Percy was about one hundred feet ahead of me, when a skoshi cab made a quick 180° turn right in front of us, and Percy hit him with full force. Percy was bleeding profusely from one knee through a torn flight suit. As I arrived on the scene, Percy was giving the guy a forgiving hug, before heading on south. I would bet he still has a chevron-shaped scar on that knee, unless what happened later as a prisoner of war obliterated it.

During our time on Okinawa, we socialized and had a lot of fun at flight parties, and even performed official duties when required. The alert pad was a rotten place to be. By 1965 we had been in Southeast Asia, actually dropping bombs, strafing, and getting shot at in the company of squadron mates, as opposed to sitting in preparedness on the pad to fly a dreadful single ship nuclear venture, if an alarm sounded. The two venues were not comparable in our minds.

Drama Over the East China Sea

by Lowell Peterson, Captain
Flight Surgeon, 12th Tactical Fighter Squadron

*Blue staff cars with colonel's or general's flags on the front are
an impressive sight as long as they are not parked in your driveway.*
Peggy Street

On a quiet Saturday afternoon in the spring of 1965, I was playing with my one-year-old daughter in the backyard of our cement-block house at Kadena Circle when the phone rang. Capt. Frank Street, the acting commander of the F-105 alert pad was on the line. "Doc, get down here right now. We need you. We need your advice. We're dealing with a serious situation." I told him I'd be there in ten minutes.

When I arrived at the 18th TFW (Tactical Fighter Wing) headquarters command post, I

Frank and Peggy Street with sons Paul and David, early 1970s

was surprised to see Colonel Cardenas, commander of the 18th Wing and the 44th TFS (Tactical Fighter Squadron) commander were also there. I was quickly briefed to the crisis and its implications. In essence, the day had started off in a routine manner when a flight of two F-105s were scheduled to fly from Kadena to Taiwan for aircraft maintenance. Lead pilot Capt. Marvin Montgomery had recently returned from combat in Vietnam, where he had received the Bronze Star and the Air Medal. His wingman, Capt. William Burkitt, was also a combat veteran.

Several minutes after takeoff, the pilots flew toward a compulsory reporting point. When the time came to call in their navigational position, Montgomery's radio remained silent. His wingman repeatedly tried to establish contact, but received no reply. After several unanswered calls, Burkitt moved his F-105

Thunderchief in for a closer look. Pulling alongside, he saw Montgomery's head was tilted back as if he were gazing at the sky, and in the next moment he observed the lead pilot's head slump forward. Burkitt concluded that Montgomery was unconscious.

The Kadena control center received Burkitt's call declaring an emergency. Two KC-135 airborne refueling tankers and a flight of F-4C interceptors were scrambled to give chase, and those of us in the command post followed the unfolding drama through radio transmissions. We heard that the flight leader's aircraft had gradually changed course and was now aimed directly at the Chinese coast. In 1965 Communist China's borders were sealed and heavily defended. Chairman Mao Tse-tung was in complete dictatorial control of this vast Red nation that had formidable military force and nuclear weapons. The threat of converting the Cold War between China and the United States into open conflict was an ongoing concern.

Montgomery's airplane was on automatic pilot, which only the man in the cockpit could disengage. The F-105s were now hundreds of miles out over the China Sea, traveling at an airspeed of MACH 0.9. With time running short, Burkitt tried to change the course of Montgomery's aircraft by lifting its left wing, but the strong stabilizing control of the autopilot would not permit this maneuver. He then positioned his Thunderchief's wing several feet forward and above the flight leader's right wing to disturb the airflow. Burkitt then began a series of slow turns, which pushed the wing down a couple of degrees for short periods of time until the autopilot again forced a correction. Despite thick cloud cover that limited visibility, Burkitt continued these maneuvers, and ultimately he was able to change the course 90 degrees.

During the flight, the F-105s had actually passed 80 miles inland over the coast of China and their flight path took them directly over the major seaport of Shanghai. The Chinese presumably scrambled fighter aircraft to give chase, but fortunately, the Chinese air defense radar system failed, and to our knowledge, no visual fighter intercept occurred. One can only imagine the communication interchanges between Washington and Beijing during this crisis, while we in the command post sat helplessly monitoring the situation.

Ed "Moose" Skowran, a 44th Squadron mate of the involved pilots, noted recently, "The Chinese blew their chance to create an international incident, but the North Koreans were waiting to take advantage of the situation." Shooting down a U.S. fighter-bomber plane—attacking (?) or spying (?) over their sovereign territory—would have been a huge propaganda coup with a major effect on international opinion.

Burkitt remained with Montgomery until the last possible moment. He then flew back to Kadena with a minimum of fuel reserve in his tanks. Later, at 18th TFW headquarters, we were informed from land-based radar units in South Korea that Captain Montgomery's plane disappeared from radar scopes while flying over the Yellow Sea, between China and Korea. Search and rescue operations in the reported impact area found no evidence of the aircraft or its pilot.

Upon landing at Kadena, the veteran fighter pilot was met by his division and wing commanders, Maj. Gen. A. P. Clark and Col. Robert Cardenas. Clearly shaken, Burkitt said, "I would've gotten out of the cockpit and walked across that wing to help Monty if it were at all possible. He was one of my best friends."

Now, it was necessary to notify Mrs. Montgomery. Peggy Street, apprised of the situation by her husband, Frank, had taken Mrs. Montgomery shopping before stopping by Marge and Ed Skowran's house for a visit. Soon after they arrived there, Colonel Cardenas, Captain Street, myself, and the chaplain came in to deliver the sad news. I told Mrs. Montgomery that in my opinion her husband had probably suffered a heart attack and cardiac arrest or a catastrophic cerebral hemorrhage. Her reaction was initially disbelief, but in seconds was replaced by overwhelming grief, tears, and screams of "No, no, no!"

I think often of that widow and the multiple USAF widows and POW wives who would suffer in the next several years of the Vietnam air war. I will always respect their courage for enduring an agony that is unimaginable and, in many cases, never-ending.

The Distinguished Flying Cross was presented to Capt. William Burkitt for his heroic efforts by Lieut. Gen. Thomas S. Moreman, Vice Commander in Chief, Pacific Air Force (PACAF).

Capt. William Burkitt (second from right) briefs (left to right): Col. Robert Cardenas, 18th Tactical Fighter Wg. commander; Maj. Gen. A. P. Clark, 313th Air Division commander; and Col. Floyd White, 18th vice commander. USAF photo

Capt. William Burkitt. USAF photo

A New Life Begins

by Lowell Peterson, Captain
Flight Surgeon, 12th Tactical Fighter Squadron
Commander, Detachment 4, 1st Medical Service Wing

During 1964-1966, Detachment 4 (Det. 4), 1st Medical Service Wing (1st Med. Svc. Wg.) had multiple deployments, mostly to Bien Hoa, South Vietnam. The three other doctors assigned to me were all single and anxious to go on TDYs (temporary duty assignments) to get away from the Kadena dispensary where they were required to see dependents and be medical officer of the day (MOD), which included night call and a 24-hour shift. I was married and had a baby daughter so the other flight surgeons would say, "You need to stay at home; we'll go." I was grateful for their generosity but sheepish about being the commander of this field dispensary unit and not pulling my weight. Captains Dick Friedman, Jerry Unatin, and John Morgan carried the load and performed in an exemplary manner. Unatin would ride in the choppers to help evacuate wounded, even carrying a sidearm .38 caliber pistol, which he did not know how to use. One day, his chopper drew fire from the enemy with bullets ricocheting off the fuselage, and the reality of being in a war zone hit home.

Jerry Unatin with Vietnamese corpsman at Bien Hoa, South Vietnam

In early 1965 members of the 12th and 67th Squadrons deployed to Da Nang, South Vietnam, and subsequently to Korat, Thailand, to begin raids into North Vietnam, Laos, and along the Ho Chi Minh Trail. No medical support from Det. 4 was requested or ordered from 1st Med. Svc. Wg., and no orders for flight surgeons to accompany the squadrons were forthcoming. At this stage of the Vietnam War, the role of the F-105s were not well defined and the targets were often suspected truck parks under heavy tree cover along the Ho Chi Minh trail. The pilots called these missions "toothpick missions". They splintered a lot of trees but rarely destroyed trucks or got secondary explosions from transported explosives.

While the F-105s and our pilots were deployed on this first TDY, I had the good fortune to catch a flight as a crew member on Maj. Gen. Albert P. Clark's C-54 en route to the Philippines where the General was to attend a conference of high brass at Baguio, a mountainous Philippine resort. General Clark was the commander of the 313th Air Division, the immediate superior to the 18th TAC Fighter Wing, under direction of 5th Air Force.

Maj. Gen. A. P. Clark,
313th Air Division
commander

The General invited me to join him for lunch even though I was trying to keep a low profile and stay out of his way. During our meal, the General began to interrogate me about military medicine and medical issues. He inquired about my responsibilities as a flight surgeon and whether I was happy in that role. I didn't have time to eat a bite, and only sipped at my coffee cup, which took all of my focus to hold steady. General Clark impressed me with his intellect and his ability to probe to the root of all issues.

He asked, "What F-105 Squadron are you attached to?"

I answered, that I was the flight surgeon for the 12th Squadron.

He hesitated only a moment, and then said in a louder, more inquisitive, and accusatory tone, "The 12th Squadron is deployed down south; why in hell aren't you with them?"

I told him that I had not received any orders to be deployed, and that because I was a member of the 1st Medical Service Wing, my orders would have to come from Colonel Dye, whose headquarters were at Clark Air Force Base in the Philippines.

General Clark leaned back in his chair, introspective, and when he made eye contact with me again, he said, "We'll see about that!" The conversation was over. I excused myself, armpits soaked, and thanked him for his hospitality.

I suspect that General Clark cornered Colonel Dye at Baguio and probably made him sweat a bit, also. From then on, when our 18th TFW squadrons deployed, we, as their flight surgeons, went with them with direct orders from 1st Medical Service Wing. From the spring of 1965 until the permanent wings were established at the bases in Thailand, this pattern of TDYs continued unbroken. It was very clear to me that my very stressful lunch and my candid conversation with the

Doc Peterson at Korat, Thailand

general had initiated the process.

In late 1965 or early 1966, Detachment 4 received orders to deploy to Phan Rang, South Vietnam. I decided that it was my turn to take a TDY to South Vietnam. My corpsmen and I, as well as all of our equipment, arrived at Naha Air Base, Okinawa, early one morning to await a C-130 that was to arrive and transport us to Southeast Asia. When the C-130 had not arrived by afternoon, we began sending a series of TWIX messages to Clark Air Force Base and to Colonel Dye's headquarters, trying to determine what had happened to our transportation. We finally got an answer late in the day and were told there would be no C-130, but no explanation was given. I found out a few days later that Phan Rang had been overrun by the Viet Cong on the day we were due to arrive there. Somebody was looking out for us, but I don't think it was our Philippine headquarters.

When I left the Air Force, I received a nice letter from Colonel Dye thanking me for my dedicated service to the success of the mission of the 1st Medical Service Wing. I found that personal touch very rewarding.

HEADQUARTERS
1ST MEDICAL SERVICE WING (PACAF)
UNITED STATES AIR FORCE
APO SAN FRANCISCO 96274

REPLY TO
ATTN OF: PNLW

SUBJECT: Letter of Appreciation

1 7 MAR 1966

TO: Capt Lowell F. Peterson, Comdr
Det 4, 1st Medical Service Wing
APO US Forces 96239

1. As we are nearing the end of our 1st Medical Service Wing relationship, I wish to express my appreciation for the excellent service you have rendered our organization. I hope that the experiences you have gained have been rewarding and will aid you in meeting future commitments. Your service as Commander of Detachment 4 has played a substantial part in furnishing medical support to Southeast Asia which otherwise would have been non-existent. You and your people are to be congratulated on the manner in which you fulfilled your assignments, always reflecting esprit de corps and dedication to the 1st Medical Service Wing mission.

2. I have sincerely enjoyed working with you and wish you success in future endeavors.

FRED C. DYE, Col, USAF, MC
Commander

KOOM

by
Lowell Peterson

The Kadena Officers Open Mess (KOOM) was the social center of the base. We called it the Officers Club, the "O" Club, or just The Club. It was where officers' wives had teas, luncheons, and played bridge, and where they took their children to the swimming pool, and worked on their tans. It was where we held welcoming parties for new arrivals and sayonara (farewell) parties for those returning to the States.

It was also the site of the officers' "dining-ins", which were rather formal all-male social events, including a cocktail party, a steak dinner, speeches by the

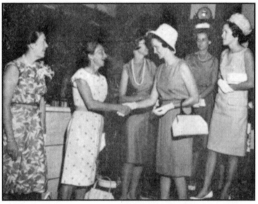

The receiving line (left to right): Mrs. Albert P. Clark, Mrs. L. Sanders, President of the KOWC, and Mrs. W. R. Hunter, 1st Vice President (last in line on the far right is Mary Peterson, the author's wife - white gloves and hats were a requirement)

top brass, and a presentation of medals to honor individuals of the 18th TAC Fighter Wing. After the award ceremony, the colonel or general in charge ordered the smoking lamp to be lit. (This was a model of an F-105 aircraft on the head table that spewed propane flames from its tail section.) While most everyone lit cigars or cigarettes and ordered more drinks, raucous entertainment, that could only be appreciated by men, was presented on stage.

The Officers Club stag bar was the place to be on Friday afternoon after duty-hours were over and the buglar's "Retreat" had been played over the base loud-speaker system. A bell with a clangor hung above the bar, and if anyone was celebrating a promotion, an award, or an impending return to the States, it was their duty to clang the bell to indicate that they were buying a round of drinks for everybody. After an hour or two, the social gathering would deteriorate into a predictably bawdy affair with singing and limericks replacing conversation. Soon enough, pangs of conscience intervened and the officers, relieved of their stress and frustration, gradually disbanded to be met at their homes by worried and angry wives.

By the time Saturday night rolled around, domestic tranquility had been restored and it was time to get the babysitter and go off to the "O" Club again, this time as couples. Tables were reserved for the various squadrons and organizations

Okinawa greets "Hello Dolly",
Mary Martin and Loring Smith

well before the weekend, and party rooms were secured for pre-dinner cocktail parties. Following cocktails, it was time to move to the squadron tables, which were arranged around the club according to rank and privilege. My wife and I were fortunate to be seated at the 12th Squadron table with the pilots and their spouses on many occasions. We dined on chateaubriand, while the in-house orchestra, Jesse Hernandez and his Boys, entertained us with old standards. Dancing followed dinner and the night usually ended by midnight.

In 1965, as the war escalated, more and more big name entertainers began to filter through Okinawa on their way to Vietnam. Comedians, singers, acting groups, and jazz combos appeared. Frankie Laine came to the Officers Club in the summer of 1965, the Kingston Trio was there in the fall, and Hello Dolly with Mary Martin was presented at the huge Stillwell Fieldhouse in October 1965. The magazine *This Week On Okinawa* noted:

> *Miss Mary Martin and a cast of* Hello Dolly *captivated audiences numbering in the thousands, as they gave five performances here this week. They faced tumultuous applause at every turn, and Miss Martin's every entrance was greeted by cheering from a crowd that filled the huge Stillwell Fieldhouse. Showing no ill effects from their recent series of one-night stands throughout Vietnam, the cast and crew gave a performance marked by a professionalism rarely seen in this remote corner of the world. The performance ended to a standing ovation by the whole audience. The applause built as the company took its bows until it changed to exuberant cheering when Miss Martin stepped to center stage. Obviously,*

deeply moved by the audience's acclaim, Miss Martin moved to the apron of the stage and sang, "Hello Okinawa!" Miss Martin was presented a traditional Okinawa Hanagusa hat by Lieutenant General Albert Watson II, as a token of Okinawa's appreciation.

Bob Hope and his traveling troupe gave an impromptu show without fanfare at one of the Marine bases in northern Okinawa on a Sunday afternoon. The word spread; we all went, and the place was packed. We savored this touch of home, and as we went back to work on Monday, Bob Hope flew off to Vietnam for another series of shows.

KINGSTON TRIO

DATE: 16 OCT 1965

TIME:

On November 19, 1965, the Kadena Officers Club was honored with the presence of Miss Patti Page. Following cocktails, we all made our way into the dining room for our chateaubriand dinner. Generals, colonels, and honored guests occupied the front-row-center tables. My wife and I

PALLADIUM PROMOTION PRESENTS

Patti Page Show

DATE: 19 NOV 1965

TIME:

PLACE: KADENA OFFICERS' OPEN MESS

sat at the 12th TAC fighter squadron table to the right of the dance floor. After dinner, as we joined in the mood of the night, Patti Page sang her multiple hits, including "How Much is that Doggie in the Window?" and "Allegheny Moon," but, everybody waited to hear her sing "Tennessee Waltz". As the night grew late and eyelids began to droop, I recall Maj. Ralph Bowersox saying, "I ain't going home 'til she sings 'Tennessee Waltz.'" Finally, she did sing "Tennessee Waltz," and was rewarded with a standing ovation.

I returned with my family to Kadena Air Force Base in 1986 and 1992. We visited Kue Hospital where my first child was born, and the Lutheran Service Center where she was baptized. We also stopped by the on-base and off-base houses where we lived. We visited the squadron areas, the base ops area, the medical dispensary, the BX, and the commissary, all of which had been so much a part of our lives for those years in the 1960s. And, of course, we went to the Officers Club.

Its appearance had not changed at all in the intervening 25 years, but when I walked in I immediately sensed a difference. The spirit was gone. It was no longer the social center of the base or of the island. New and elegant Japanese hotels and resorts now dotted the entire island of Okinawa, offering excellent restaurants and entertainment venues. I felt a bit sad as I rambled through the deserted stag bar and stood in the dining room near the stage. In that moment I could visualize, once again, the men of the 12th Squadron and Major Bowersox sitting on the first elevation on the right flank, as Miss Patti Page sang "The Tennessee Waltz".

I was dancing with my darling to the Tennessee Waltz ....

SAC

by
Lowell Peterson

My wife and I were at the Kadena Officers Club for dinner on a Saturday night in late 1965 when Maj. Bob Bonner, who was my immediate superior in the flight surgeon office at Kadena Air Force Base (AFB), came by our table late in the evening, leaned over, and told me in hushed tones, "SAC is coming." He had just been at a 313th Air Division briefing by Gen. A. P. Clark, who had informed those present that the 7th Air Refueling Squadron of the 4252nd Strategic Wing of the Strategic Air Command (SAC) was going to arrive at Kadena AFB later that evening. This SAC Wing, known as the Young Tiger Unit flew KC-135 stratotankers (Boeing 707 airplanes configured to be flying gas tanks). He said that if I wanted to see something really impressive, I should be at the west end of the runway at Kadena at midnight, when they were due to arrive.

My wife and I left the Club at 11:30, drove to the end of the runway alongside of Highway 1. Right at midnight, the first tanker was seen on its approach. Highway 1 is so close to the end of the runway that when the planes landed, they were only fifty to one hundred feet above the highway. We got out of the car and stood there as the whole squadron landed, one after another, thirty seconds apart. It was absolutely awesome to watch, and the noise from their four jet engines was deafening.

In the days and years to come, these airplanes would leave Okinawa, once or twice per day, loaded to the gills with JP-4 jet fuel, so heavy they barely could make it off the end of the ten-thousand-foot runway. Their mission was primarily to refuel fighter-bombers, including those of our own 18th TFW, which were engaged in combat bombing missions over North Vietnam. Kadena AFB had taken another step in being a major player in the war.

KC-135 inflight refueling plane (Boeing 707)

Hong Kong
by
Lowell Peterson

Hong Kong from the Peak, 1965

Every so often one had to get off "The Rock" (Okinawa). Veterans of the base knew this all too well, which is why they informed me on my first day on the island that I needed to sign-up for the Officer's Wives Club R&R (rest and relaxation) flight to Hong Kong. It didn't matter that my wife and I wouldn't need a vacation for months. The USAF courtesy flight came with a waiting list that was at least that long. So, Monday morning saw me at the appropriate desk filling out the appropriate forms, securing my wife and me a place aboard a C-54 for a future vacation.

When our time finally came, we joined about fifteen other couples for our vacation to Hong Kong. Because I was on "flying status", I had already made numerous trips to the city as a crew member on these R&R trips. After we arrived at Kai-tak airport and checked into the President Hotel in Kowloon, the wives immediately began a shopping tour, acquiring pearls, jade, ivory carvings, cameras, furniture, clothes, and shoes. What could not be found in Kowloon could certainly be found on Hong Kong Island, a quick trip away on the Star Ferry.

Of course, everyone wanted to go sightseeing, and there was no better place in the world to do it. The beautiful harbor was visible from almost any point on either Hong

Kong Island or Kowloon. The Chinese junks, with their rectangular hulls and square sails, silently moved back and forth through the harbor, delivering their goods and giving us all a beautiful picture to remember. We walked through back-street open-air markets where the local people bought their food. Dressed chickens and slabs of beef and pork hung from hooks, while the counters overflowed with every

Rice paddies—Communist China, north of Hong Kong, 1965

kind of vegetable. Large burlap sacks of rice were everywhere, and we even saw the so-called thousand-year-old eggs that had been buried in mud.

A trip through farmland and rice paddies north of Hong Kong into what is called the New Territories, to the sealed border of Communist Red China, brought forth ominous thoughts about the Cold War world in which we lived. A ride in a Mercedes taxi (all taxis in Hong Kong were Mercedes) around Hong Kong Island to Aberdeen revealed the "boat people" as they are called, living on their small boats all tied together in the harbor. They walked on planks from one boat to another to get to their "home". Fish were drying in the sun on racks, giving this area its own unique atmosphere and smell.

Feeling adventurous, my wife and I made arrangements through the American and Portuguese embassies to take a hydrofoil trip to Macau, the Portuguese colony an hour away from Hong Kong. This peninsula colony, noted for its gambling casinos, was only 100 yards or so from mainland China. On our taxi tour we saw children less than six years old, making firecrackers by the gross while their parents fished in waters strewn with abandoned military craft used to evacuate Chinese Nationalists ahead of Mao's advancing armies in 1949. Because we were there in October, there were huge banners and billboards over the streets and on public buildings celebrating Mao and the communist revolution. The charged political atmosphere, not to mention the armed Chinese military guards who were clearly visible, made our sightseeing trip more than a little intimidating. A walk through the gambling casino, with its steely-eyed security guards and solemn, bald-headed Chinese croupiers put the final scare into

Star Ferry, Hong Kong

my wife, and we headed back to the dock to return to Hong Kong.

When we returned, it was time to have afternoon tea at the top of the Hilton Hotel. Then we boarded the tram to climb to "the Peak", the highest point on Hong Kong. From there the entire harbor and all of Kowloon spread out in front of us. It was majestic. In the evening we dressed for dinner and prepared to enjoy the best cuisine from every part of the world. Would it be a multi-course meal at Gaddi's, the Peninsula Hotel, or the Carlton Hotel, which might consist of escargot, French onion soup, an elegant seafood entrée, salad, and dessert or would we venture to a floating Chinese restaurant in the harbor serving succulent broiled lobsters? For us, who had grown up in rural Wisconsin, these dining experiences were a gourmet revelation. We never wanted to leave.

When the sun went down, we watched the junks move slowly through the moon-lit harbor, and then retired to the Firecracker Bar, secluded in the underground reaches of the President Hotel. There, the drinks were good and the entertainment fabulous. A family group named The Reynettes provided the music. They were very good! On many occasions we sat there for hours, sipping our drinks, listening to their renditions of American favorites. The lead singer, Luz Vi Minda, had a voice that was a combination of Connie Francis and Leslie Gore at their best. I loved to hear her sing

one of the band's own creations called, "Hong Kong, Downtown Hong Kong". It was a magical time.

I took my family back to Hong Kong in 1992 because I wanted to share the city I loved above all others once more with my wife and to introduce it to my children. The city and the harbor were just as amazing and the view from the Peak was as breathtaking as ever. I returned to Lee Kee's custom shoe shop, where I had a pair of shoes made in 1965, and asked Lee Kee if he still had the pattern. Sure enough, he went into his back room and came out with a large catalog of footprints drawn on each page, including mine. I put my foot down on the page and it fit, so I ordered another pair of shoes. The times I shared with Air Force friends and my wife in this beautiful city and the evenings in the Firecracker Bar were special, and something that I will always treasure.

The Reynettes

Flying Time
by
Lowell Peterson

During 1964 through 1966, I was privileged to receive many hours of flying time at Kadena Air Force Base with flights originating from Base Flight Operations under the direction of Maj. Joe Banks. In addition to the C-47 and C-54 flights to the Philippines, Hong Kong, Taiwan, and Japan, I was able to fly in the T-39 twin-engine jet and the T-33 two-seat single engine jet trainer.

Doc Peterson

The T-39 was a comfortable business jet that was used for multiple purposes. Pilots who flew this aircraft maintained their proficiency and also checked out pilots who wished to upgrade from single engine to twin-engine jet aircraft. The passenger area had four comfortable airliner seats. I

T-33 Jet Trainer

could sit back and read medical journals while the pilot and his student copilot practiced repeated touch-and-go take-offs and landings. I thought this was all rather routine until one day when the student pilot almost ran off the right side of the runway before his instructor took over and got us airborne again. I realized that a little too much power on one engine and not enough rudder control might cause that result. On another occasion, the pilot and student copilot were practicing stalls by putting the nose up and the power down. It is a disconcerting feeling to suddenly go to this nose up attitude and not hear any engine noise. I was always thankful to feel the nose go down and hear the engines come to life.

We used the T-39 to fly faker missions to test the air defenses of Okinawa. We flew due west about two hundred miles, turned around, and flew directly back to Okinawa at 45,000 feet. The F-4Cs stationed at Naha Air Base were supposed to scramble and intercept us. For some unknown reason, there was no scramble and no intercept. We flew directly over the island, and nobody paid any attention to us. At

T-39

that moment, I felt that our military forces on Okinawa were a bit vulnerable, even though I had always felt we were just the opposite— invulnerable. The best part of that trip for me was the opportunity to sit in the copilot seat for much of the trip.

We also used the T-39 early in 1965 for an emergency mission to Clark Air Force Base in the Philippines to deliver Col. Robinson Risner's dress blue uniform, so that it would be waiting for him when he arrived from Korat Air Force Base to catch a commercial flight to Washington, DC. He had been summoned to the Pentagon by the Defense Department, to report on the progress of the air war over North Vietnam. Obviously, he had no need for a dress blue uniform in a combat zone, but when the Pentagon requested his presence, the situation changed suddenly and dramatically.

In contrast to the comfortable T-39, the T-33 is a two-seat-in-tandem, single-engine jet trainer, primarily used for the purpose of keeping jet pilots proficient, even though their current duty assignment on the base was not an active flying position. It was also used to upgrade propeller-driven reciprocating engine pilots to jet proficiency. I was able to log a lot of flying time in the back seat of the T-33. Normally, these were routine flights for the pilots to acquire flying time and make touch-and-go landings and takeoffs. The pilot would also use this time to practice combat maneuvers, aerobatics, and whatever he could to "wring-out" the doc in the backseat. I usually could hold my own pretty well without getting sick, but on occasion, after an hour or so of high-grade stress to my vestibular system, I would request to be taken back to the base. This option seemed preferable to vomiting into my gloves or my helmet.

I often had very thoughtful pilots who took my well-being into consideration and actually tried to teach me something about flying. One time, well out over the ocean, away from any sight of land, the pilot allowed me to fly the T-33. I did pretty well at staying level and not wandering off course, but I had to concentrate vigorously on the instruments in the cockpit and not be gazing about. He then allowed me to make some aileron rolls, learning how to keep the nose up when the wings were in a vertical position before rolling out upright again. Of course, I did this while watching the instruments in the cockpit. After congratulating me for my efforts, clumsy as they may have been, the pilot asked if I wished to make one more roll prior to returning to base. Of course, I acknowledged in the affirmative. I went ahead and made the aileron roll and was really pleased with my effort, when the pilot said, "Don't you think you ought to roll it the rest of the way?" I looked out of the cockpit and saw what I believed to be blue sky above me. I was confused momentarily until I realized I was looking at the ocean far below. Embarrassed, I rolled the rest of the way until I had the true blue sky above me. The pilot laughed, eased my embarrassment with some comforting words, and turned the T-33 toward Kadena Air Base. Years later, in 1988, as I was about to go under anesthesia for coronary bypass surgery, the operating room nurses told me I had related the story of my upside down flight to them as my final words before the anesthetic took total control. They apparently got quite a laugh out of it, just like the pilot had those many years before. They did not relate this story to me until several years later because they could not believe that it was possibly true.

Always trying for flying time, I took the opportunity to go to Naha Air Base and catch a flight on a Navy C-130 to Atzugi Air Base near Yokahama, Japan. The Navy pilots were very gracious in allowing me aboard for this round-trip flight. I looked forward to it because I had never been to this area of Japan. We were on the ground at Atzugi long enough for me to visit the Base Exchange and buy a stereo receiver. Back on board with my treasured purchase, we soon were airborne. The cargo hold of the fuselage was now empty as we returned to Okinawa. On the way back, I inquired what cargo we had carried to Japan. I was informed the entire cargo hold on our outgoing leg had been filled with defective rocket motors. I decided then and there that I probably should continue to fly only with the Air Force.

*Doc and F-105 prior to a flight with
Captain Charlie Copin*

As interesting as these flying experiences were, nothing could compare with my flights in the rear seat of the F-105F. The pre-flight briefing with the 12th TFS pilots—donning G-suit, parachute, and helmet—was followed by a pre-flight inspection of the airplane before the crew chief strapped me into the back seat.

Starting engine, taxiing, arming the ordnance at the end of the runway in preparation for takeoff, progressively increased my level of excitement. I had no emotion of fear. There was complete confidence in the pilot and in the awesomely powerful machine in whose confines I now sat. The mind-boggling thrust unleashed at takeoff in afterburner, provided the greatest endorphin high I have ever experienced. When we were at altitude, the flight to the bombing range was smooth as silk and I got to fly the airplane for a short time.

One of the missions involved shooting pods of 19 rockets at a target during a steep dive, which was like watching an entire July 4th fireworks show go off in the flash of an eye.

Other missions involved simulated nuclear toss-bombing at an island target. The approach to the target was at fifty feet above the ocean at 0.9 MACH followed by a sudden gut-wrenching pitch-up at a steep angle to a computer identified bomb release point, and then a sharp left turn at high G-force to clear the area. These repeated attack approaches (we made several) gave me a sense of appreciation of what pilots experienced in their combat runs at targets in North Vietnam. The only difference was that here, no one was shooting at us.

A Flight on a Gooney Bird

by
Lowell Peterson

C-47

It was supposed to be a routine flight; a quick hop over to Taipei, Taiwan, from Okinawa in a C-47 "Gooney Bird"—a two-engine propeller plane of World War II vintage. The mission was to deliver some very expensive, highly-sensitive instruments with top-secret capabilities that were being guarded by an Air Force second lieutenant. I received a call from Capt. Joe Banks at Base Flight operations asking if I wanted to go along. Of course I said "yes," because I needed the flying time and I was always eager to fly with his crews.

He said, "The plane leaves in one hour; get down here ASAP."

I called my wife, told her to pack my suitcase and meet me in thirty minutes at Base Ops.

With all of the high-tech multi-million dollar planes taking off and landing, our old C-47 Dakota did not cause a blink of an eye. The crew consisted of our pilot, copilot, flight engineer, and crew chief, a nervous twenty-one-year-old airman first-class bucking for sergeant's stripes. The lieutenant and I were the only passengers on board, and the only cargo was the mysterious top-secret box of instruments, four-foot square and one-foot deep, resting in the middle of the cargo bay.

The first half of the flight was uneventful, and I settled in to read some medical journals. The lieutenant and I chatted intermittently, but he did not say much about his instruments, except that they were very expensive and that he was responsible for their safe delivery. After awhile I stared out the window as the aircraft droned on over a seemingly endless East China Sea, devoid of ships, islands, or any point of orientation. I silently marveled at the vast expanse of the ocean below. Suddenly, I glimpsed something out of the corner of my eye that jolted me upright. I saw oil, black engine oil, streaming in rivulets over the right wing. I had no more whispered to myself that this was not good, when I saw the propeller freeze and heard the engine shutdown. I thought, "Oh, shit, is this it?"

In the next moment, the cockpit erupted in frantic activity. Many "May-day" radio calls were made as we lost altitude. The pilot was able to level the clumsy plane out at four thousand feet and climb back up, but when he reached eight thousand feet, the single remaining engine started to overheat. So, he backed off power and gradually descended once again to four thousand feet. After we repeated these up-and-down maneuvers a few times, the pilot ordered the crew chief to throw out all nonessential baggage. The airman first-class, grabbing a rope, tied himself to a supporting structure of the fuselage and opened the rear cargo door. The rush of air past the open door was deafening. The first thing he grabbed was the box of the lieutenant's expensive, and possibly irreplaceable instruments. I can still see the anguished look on the young lieutenant's face, as he begged the airman first class not to jettison the valuable box he had babied for weeks. The airman threw it out anyway, and the young lieutenant, with no recourse, watched his USAF career sink into the deep along with the box. My suitcase was next. There may be still some marine mammal out there in the Pacific wearing jockey shorts. Then, the airman threw out the parachutes. Well, that did it. I figured we were toast. There was nothing out there but the sky above and the vast sea below, and we hung suspended in between by one engine.

Meanwhile, a C-130 cargo plane had heard our distress call and was able to locate us. The sight of that C-130 was a relief, but in reality, I had a false sense of security as there was nothing its crew could do except observe our fate. Our crew decided on the flight deck that there was no way we could get into Taipai, Taiwan, because we could not fly higher than eight thousand feet without the engine overheating, and the mountains surrounding the Taipei Airport stood at twelve thousand feet. Therefore, the pilot turned the plane around and began to fly back toward Okinawa with our C-130 escort. We were a long way from anywhere, and our fate was not at all clear.

Rather than take a chance on making it another 150 miles back to Okinawa, the pilot decided to land on the island of Miyako-jima. I was relieved that we had a plan, but I was not convinced this fly-speck of an island would prove to be our salvation. After what seemed to be an interminable time period, we began our approach to the dirt airstrip. For me, this was scary, but for the pilot and copilot it must have been a nightmare, trying to adjust airspeed, drag, altitude, and rudder control on their single-engine-powered aircraft. We approached and landed, kicking-up a huge cloud of dust, blotting out the horizon. This, along with the noise of the spraying gravel, the creaking fuselage, and the wind whipping past the open cargo door made everything seem surreal. As the dust cleared and the aircraft slowed, it became apparent we were down, and I finally exhaled. Our Day of Judgment had not come.

Nerves shot, we impatiently exited the airplane through the open door and saw that the C-130 was also coming in for a landing. I think their crew saw this as a challenge and possibly a reason for decoration. The tsunami of dust created by the multi-engine C-130, several times larger than the C-47, was spectacular. We gladly climbed aboard the C-130, abandoned the C-47, and in a cloud of dust and a hearty "Hi-Ho Silver," took off for Okinawa.

Later that evening, I walked into my house to the amazement of my wife, who said, "I thought you went to Taiwan."

I replied, "Honey, it's a long story, but my suitcase didn't make it back."

The airman first class was demoted to airman third class, from three stripes to one stripe for jettisoning life saving equipment—the parachutes. His aspiring Air Force career was over. The pilot was recognized for his salvage of the airplane, but not for complete command and control of his crew and responsibility. He was asked to retire. His flying days were over. I don't know what happened to the young lieutenant, but I was sure he would survive, Air Force or no Air Force. As for me, I went back to work, happy to have survived this experience. Facing my mortality eight thousand feet in the air convinced me that fate, luck, divinity, and, "It's just not your time to go," are very real concepts. It also gave me a better understanding for the pilots of the 12th TAC fighter squadron, and for the uncertainty they faced day after day on missions over North Vietnam and Laos, never knowing their fate. I often heard them say after returning, "Well, we cheated death again today!"

And, after my trip on the "Gooney Bird," I think I know what they meant.

Survival Training

by
Lowell Peterson

Webster defines "survival" as "remaining alive or in existence, to continue life or activity, or to outlive." In time of war, there is no more powerful instinct. War is about survival—me or him, them or us, our nation or theirs, our culture or theirs, and all too often, our religion or theirs.

In the military, special survival training is required for everyone who will walk in harm's way, including flight surgeons. I had ejection seat and parachute training. The latter involved jumping to the ground from two-foot and four-foot platforms, and then swinging in a harness from a twenty-foot platform and being dropped to earth by ropes and pulleys to learn how to make a parachute landing fall (PLF). I was also pulled in the harness across rough ground behind a tractor so I could practice disengaging from the chute using the quick-release device. After an entire day of jumping and dragging, I can truthfully say that I was never so sore in my life. The morning after, I could only roll out of bed on my hands and knees, and then had to be helped to my feet.

Sea Survival School off the coast of Okinawa was physically less demanding because water is a bit more forgiving than terra firma. But psychologically, the sea was brutal. Experiences like jumping out of a helicopter into the ocean, getting pulled behind a boat while trying to unhitch parachute harness straps, and being momentarily trapped under a parachute canopy while treading water, were frightening enough to make me wish I were still being dragged behind a tractor. Another test involved being crammed in a so-called twenty-man life raft filled to capacity, while an evasion-colored tarpaulin covered us. I can still feel the stifling heat and the endless rocking as we sat eating C-rations between bouts of nausea. This was not my idea of a picnic! Being in a one-man life raft, well away from the mother ship, was no better. The loneliness, vulnerability to the sun and saltwater, as well as the threat of shark attack, gave me a deeper understanding of what many pilots actually faced.

The pilots were also required to go to jungle survival school in the Philippines,

Mexico, or Central America. They referred to it as "snake school". I was happy to be passed over for that one!

The most difficult of all survival schools, however, was the Escape and Evasion School. It also taught our fliers about enemy POW interrogation techniques. I did not have to attend this school, but in retrospect I wish I had, if only to gain more insight into what a number of our pilots endured. Along with learning how to evade or escape capture and how to survive in the wild, this school instructed its students how to respond to capture and torture by the enemy. It was a grueling two weeks of intense pressure, meant to toughen the body and the mind.

At a recent reunion of the River Rats (Red River Valley Fighter Pilot Assoc.), I discussed this training ground with Chuck Hofelich, a former 12th TFS pilot. I told him that I was absolutely amazed that anyone who was captured and tortured by the North Vietnamese for weeks, months, and years survived. I asked him if he thought this school helped the pilots survive.

"I'm sure that it helped," he replied. "But when you are at school, you know it is going to be over in two weeks." Those who became prisoners did not know if it would ever end. Yet, they persevered, and most did survive, although their lives were changed forever. Bob "Percy" Purcell recently described his experience as, "The war that never ends."

Sidewinder

by

Lowell Peterson

"Doc, wake up! Come on, quick! Something's happened out on the flightline. We've got to get out there!" We had very few real emergencies during our TDY (temporary duty assignment) at Korat Air Force Base, Thailand, but this sounded serious.

My adrenaline level hit max-peak in no time flat. I sprang out of bed, whipped on my fatigue pants, grabbed my boots, and ran to the ambulance on the heels of my corpsman. We were underway in seconds, with red lights rotating and sirens echoing into the night. We traversed the flat, high plain down the gravel road to the flightline, a quarter of a mile away from the base, in record time for an old "meat-wagon" ambulance, not much changed from World War II. The flightline was illuminated with floodlights, as was usual every night, while dedicated airmen and sergeants armed the airplanes for the next day's sorties. I put on my shoes en route and slipped on my fatigue shirt, buttoning it, but did not have time to tuck it in.

As we reached the flightline, we saw smoke rising near the squadron operations briefing building, where the pilots normally picked up their helmets, parachutes, personal weapons, and survival vests, and did their pre-sortie briefings and post-sortie debriefings. I couldn't believe what I saw. There, sticking out of the wall of the building, was a sidewinder air-to-air, heat-seeking missile, half-in and half-out, smoking and making a hissing noise. Airmen stood around not knowing what to do, not knowing if the missile would explode. They should have taken cover, but were too stunned to do so. I was not sure I knew how to react, either.

I inquired as to what had happened and learned that the crews had been arming the planes and as usual one noncommissioned officer was in the cockpit and one was on the ground while they carefully attached the weaponry and electronic wiring, and set up the weapon systems. This time, however, someone pushed the wrong button, or a short in the electrical system had occurred and all of a sudden the sidewinder, attached to the outer pylon of the wing of an F-105, took off at supersonic speed and impaled in the wall of the operations building.

We soon determined no one had been injured and that the demolition and weaponry people could deal with this situation. Before we returned to base, a sergeant I knew came up to me, laughing like hell, which seemed a bit inappropriate after this near disaster. I asked him what was so funny. He said that a young airman had decided to sneak off and catch a nap in a two-ton truck parked near the flightline. Because it was hot, even in the middle of the night, he left the door of the truck open as he settled down on the seat with his legs hanging out the door. When the sidewinder released, it glanced off the truck's door, tearing it off and scaring the living Jesus out of the airman. The last anyone saw of the guy, he was running through the sagebrush, across the plain, oblivious to cobras, kraits, or any other threat to his well-being. We all had a big belly laugh about the whole thing. Then my corpsmen and I returned to base to get some sleep before it was time to get up and support the pilots as they readied for another day of stress and tension in the skies over Southeast Asia.

Ghostly Flight
by
Lowell Peterson

On a warm August evening in the summer of 1965, I received an urgent telephone call at the Korat Air Force Base field medical dispensary from the duty officer at Base Ops (base operations). The officer quickly informed me that the control tower at Korat had just received a call from an unidentified aircraft requesting privilege to land. Despite repeated attempts by the tower to obtain identification of the inbound flight, there was no more information forthcoming, other than the pilot volunteering, "We have wounded aboard."

The duty officer had notified his superiors all the way up the line, and had alerted the Air Police to seal off the field and to escort the plane when it did land. He requested we bring all of our ambulances and corpsmen to the flightline and notify the army hospital that we needed possible backup. I only had two ambulances and three corpsmen, but I decided to wait it out, pending further information that would indicate the need to call for army ambulances to back us up.

The corpsmen loved the suspense and the chance to drive the quarter-mile trip to the flightline, with red lights rotating and sirens howling. I knew it was not necessary, but I let them have their fun. Once our units were in place, along with the heavily armed air police, we did what everybody did—we waited. Finally, we saw the landing lights of the plane on final approach, but still no further identity was forthcoming. The air police, red lights flashing against an onyx sky, followed the plane down the runway as it landed. The plane was totally devoid of markings; no lights on top, none on the wings, and none on the tail. An air police jeep, with a rotating white light, escorted the plane, now clearly identifiable as an American-made C-47, to a parking area, close, but not too close, to Base Ops. The C-47 was painted totally gray-black and remained as mysterious on the ground as it had been in the air.

As the air police surrounded the plane, the pilot shut down the engines and we all waited in anticipation as the rear door opened, revealing a dark interior. Soon, a tall blond American man with a T-shirt, khaki shorts, and sandals appeared and asked for the medical personnel to come aboard. My corpsmen and I entered the fuselage. The sight we beheld is burned in my memory. The bay of the plane was dimly lighted, almost totally dark, and in this abyss we saw body movements like ants on an anthill. There were several young men with straight black hair, apprehensive faces, and scraggly, never-shaven adolescent beards. They weren't wearing shirts, had only shorts or loincloths, and many were barefoot. The American volunteered that these were Hmong troops who had been involved in a firefight with the communist Pathet Lao in Laos and that several had been wounded. The dead had been left to be buried by their mountain tribesmen.

My corpsmen and I attempted a triage of sorts and took the litter cases into the ambulances, securing them in place. The walking wounded rode in the back of the ambulances or in our trucks as we proceeded with the air police escorting us to the army hospital.

The army surgeon in charge was totally ineffective. He kept saying that we needed to triage, yelling and screaming orders, and scaring the hell out of our newly-arrived patients. Finally, order was restored by calmer, rational medics, and our patients were off to x-ray and treatment rooms. Most of the combatants only required minor suturing and dressing of wounds, but I clearly remember one Laotian Hmong who had been shot through the face. His left cheek was torn apart, several teeth had been blown away, and his mandible had been fractured. On his x-ray, on the right side of his neck, was a radiodense object, the bullet, which, totally spent, had lodged just next to his carotid artery. Little did he know how close he had come to joining those of his compatriots now with the spirits of their ancestors.

The patients remained at the army hospital for several days and then were returned to the hilltops of Laos by the mysterious gray-black plane and its crew of American "cowboy" pilots (Air America was a CIA operation, supporting covert operations in North Vietnam and Laos). For my corpsmen and me, this had been an exciting and sobering experience, which made it very clear to us that the war was expanding and coming ever closer.

The Hmong tribesmen of Laos were not only fighting the Pathet Lao communists for the freedom of their country, but were also assisting our government in covert operations directed by the CIA. They were providing safe haven for U.S. airmen shot down and rescued from the dense tropical forests of Laos and North Vietnam. We owed them our respect then, and we owe them our respect now.

Singapore

by
Lowell Peterson

On a Monday morning, shortly after I arrived at the flight surgeon's office, the Senior Master Sergeant in charge informed me, "Captain, you're requested to report to 18th Tactical Fighter Wing (TFW) headquarters at 0700 on September 1, 1965, for a special briefing."

I put aside my fears of where this was going to take me—we were at war and the options were many. I did not discuss it further with my wife or my medical colleagues.

TEMPORARY DUTY ORDER—MILITARY				DATE 17 September 65
(If more space is required, continue on reverse, identifying items by number)				
TO: Hq 18 Tac Ftr Wg (18AS)		FROM: Hq 18 Tac Ftr Wg (18DCOT)		1. INDIVIDUAL(S) WP ON TDY AS SHOWN IN ITEMS 5 THROUGH 21.
2. TYPED NAME, GRADE AND TITLE OF ORDERS ISSUING OFFICIAL C E ANDERSON, Colonel, USAF Deputy Commander for Operations		3. SIGNATURE		4. PHONE NO. 41203
5. GRADE	6. NAME *(Last, first, middle initial, AFSN)*		7. ORGANIZATION	8. SECURITY CLEARANCE
COL	CARDENAS ROBERT L, 5C56A (J17)		18 Tac Ftr Wg	TOP SECRET
MAJ	HOSMER WILLIAM J, 25123A (J20)		12 Tac Ftr Sq	TOP SECRET
CAPT	SEMENOV ANATOLE JR, A03064899 (J20)		12 Tac Ftr Sq	TOP SECRET
	(See reverse side)			
9. EFFECTIVE ON OR ABOUT 18 Sep 65	10. APPROXIMATE NO. OF DAYS *(Include travel time)* 10		11. 0	DDALV
12. PURPOSE OF TDY In support of 313AD OPORD 342-66	13. ITINERARY FROM: Kadena AB APO 96239		VARIATIONS AUTHORIZED	
	TO: Tengah RAF, Singapore			
	RETURN TO: Kadena AB APO 96239			
14. MODES OF TRANSPORTATION AUTHORIZED WITHIN CONUS				

CAPT	JONES JOHN C, A03064899	(J20)	12 Tac Ftr Sq	TOP SECRET	
CAPT	REHM JOHN F, 72006A	(J20)	12 Tac Ftr Sq	TOP SECRET	
CAPT	CAREY WESLEY G JR, 68669A	(J20)	12 Tac Ftr Sq	TOP SECRET	
CAPT	STREET JAMES F, A02246276	(J17)	18 Tac Ftr Wg	TOP SECRET	
1ST LT	HOFELICH CHARLES G JR, A03122498	(J20)	12 Tac Ftr Sq	TOP SECRET	
A2C	BELTON HERBERT L JR, AF1378910	(J20)	12 Tac Ftr Sq	TOP SECRET	
*CAPT	PETERSON LOWELL F, A03126846		Det 4 1st Med Svc Wg	SECRET	

Fortunately, Col. C. E. Anderson, deputy commander for Operations, made the briefing just that—brief. He informed us that Lima Flight of the 12th TAC Fighter Squadron (TFS), myself, and support personnel would be deployed on September 8, 1965, to Tengah Royal Air Force (RAF) base, Singapore, in support of a 313th Air Division joint exercise with the RAF of Great Britain, and that we would also be closely involved with the Australian Air Force, which was also stationed at Tengah. The exercise would last ten days, and we were to be on our best behavior. The United States Air Force wished to showcase its military might to our allies, and to enhance world opinion for our mission in the Vietnam War.

Singapore is an independent island nation lying off the lower tip of the Malaysian Peninsula where the South China Sea meets the Indian Ocean. It is hard to comprehend the size of the Pacific Ocean and all its contiguous seas that extend ten thousand miles from the west coast of the U.S. to Southeast Asia, Malaysia, and India. The trip from Okinawa, past the Philippines and the Indonesian islands, was seemingly endless for me, riding in the cargo bay of a noisy C-130.

When our plane finally landed at Tengah, the F-105s were already there. The pilots of the 12th seemed grateful that I was able to join them on this TDY, and I was ecstatic. My wife, back at Kadena AFB was less than ecstatic that I was absent that evening for our 3rd wedding anniversary and a promised night out for dinner at the Officers Club.

Our first exposure to British culture was a rugby game between RAF squadrons. I had never seen a rugby game and was not prepared for the mayhem. There was blood on everybody! Teeth were loosened, eyes were swollen, and ankles gave way. The Brits invited us to join in.

Our answer was, "How about a game of softball?"

During the game, one of the 45th RAF Squadron pilots coaching his team yelled out, "Come on lads! You're playing like a bunch of tits. Pick it up, pick it up!"

This drew a few laughs from us, and a reprimanding glance from the RAF Commander. After the game, we retreated to the pub, and Yank and Brit alike got drunk on pints of beer, sang drinking songs, and affirmed the bond between our two cultures.

The following morning, after breakfast, it was time to, "Saddle up and fly." A combined exercise plan had been arranged by the British and U.S. commanders directing attacks on islands that were used for gunnery practice. The RAF flew the Canberra bomber, and the U.S. flew their 105s. Later in the exercise, there was opportunity for the Yanks to fly in a Canberra and the RAF flyers to get rides in the back seat of the F-105. I set up my clinic each morning by bringing my black medical bag to the flightline, sitting on it, and watching the planes take off and land.

Rarely did anyone come by for anything, and then it was usually for some antacid tablets or aspirin.

I was invited to dinner at the senior British doctor's house one evening, which was also attended by the other British doctors assigned to the base. It was a delightful evening and I presented them with a large bottle of Kentucky bourbon. I am sure they preferred their native single-malt Scotch whiskey, but they were very gracious in accepting my gift. The following day, the senior doctor took me on a tour of Singapore, including a visit to Changi Air Base, where I took a picture of a restored World War II British Spitfire in pristine condition. Changi was captured by the Japanese in World War II and became a POW death camp for the British. It is immortalized in James Clavell's book, *King Rat*.

Tom Lockhart in mess dress uniform

On another evening, the British pilots and their wives hosted a formal banquet for us and the Australians. We all wore our mess dress uniforms, and everyone was dressed "to the nines". After the dinner, there was entertainment and dancing. The single British and Australian pilots had recruited some BOAC (British Overseas Airway Carrier) stewardesses to the party, and they certainly livened up the affair. They were interested in my shoulder boards with my captain's bars, from my white mess dress jacket. I personally accommodated them by attaching them to the shoulder straps of their dresses. When I returned to Okinawa, I had a hard time explaining to my wife why my jacket no longer carried my rank. It's amazing what one person can do for international relations. And, so much for being on my best behavior!

On Saturday night, we went to downtown Singapore where we walked the streets, explored the thieves' alleys, bought gifts of pewter to take home, and sat at an outside cafe watching the transvestites parade about. I guarantee you, I could not tell which women were really women. It boggled my mind!

On Sunday morning, nursing hangovers, we all made ourselves presentable and attended a Sunday brunch social at the residence of the American air attaché's house. It was at a beautiful hillside location, with a view across the Singapore countryside. The house was stupendous, and the socializing and food were equally excellent. We were served many fresh fruits, and chicken satay with spicy peanut sauce.

On Monday morning, Maj. Bill Hosmer of the 12th Squadron gave an extensive briefing for the British and Australian pilots about the USAF role in the North Vietnam Air War. None of the U.S. pilots attended, as they knew the subject only too well. I had nothing else to do and was interested to hear what Major Hosmer would have to say. I stood in the back of the briefing room while he went through the details, utilizing target maps of North Vietnam and Laos, explaining the war our pilots were being asked to fight in the air from our bases in Thailand. I was stunned and shocked, but extremely honored, when at the end of his briefing, he looked at me in the back of the room and said, "Doc, have I covered everything? Can you think of anything else that I should add?"

With all of the British and Aussie pilots turning around to look at me, I answered, "No, sir, your briefing was extremely thorough and detailed." As I walked out of the briefing room, my knees were weak.

On the following day, September 17, 1965, the 313th Air Division and 18th TFW personnel were notified from Korat, Thailand, that Col. Robinson "Robbie" Risner, the 67th TFS commander, had been shot down over North Vietnam and was presumed captured and a prisoner of war.

Everybody was totally depressed. Colonel Risner was the charismatic leader of the 67th Squadron, which had replaced our 12th Squadron at Korat at the end of August 1965. He was revered by all of the 18th TFW squadrons as a combat leader who had experienced three wars and was looked up to as their acknowledged ideal leader in this conflict.

Col. Robert Cardenas, the 18th TAC Fighter Wing commander, decided he needed to go from Singapore to Korat and assume command of the 67th Squadron. He and another pilot left for Korat that afternoon in two F-105 planes. Watching them take off embedded in my mind how significant this war was and how great a loss we had suffered.

Marines

by
Lowell Peterson

The most difficult and emotional flight I ever took was a Continental Airlines Boeing 707 flight from Kadena Air Force Base (AFB), Okinawa to Da Nang AFB, South Vietnam. This flight had originated in the United States and was making a refueling stop at Kadena prior to making the final leg of its journey. Because it would return to Kadena and refuel again before returning to the United States, it was an ideal flight for me to hitch a ride on. After introducing me to the crew, the pilot asked if I would like to ride in the cockpit, as the radio operator's seat was vacant. Of course I jumped at the chance. I had never had the opportunity to be in the cockpit of a large,

```
                    1505TH SUPPORT SQUADRON (T)(MATS)
                         United States Air Force
                    APO San Francisco 96239 California


  FLIGHT ORDER
  NUMBER      ( 2-3  )

                                                  DATE: 2 Mar 66


  1.  FNP, WP o/a 2 Mar 66              , from Kadena AB, Okinawa to

  ___DANANG AD VIETNAM AND RETURN____, on TDY, for approximately 2 DAYS
  days to perform a MATS route familiarization msn, as reqd in MM 55-3
  paragraph 5-5d (32) and return to proper sta upon comp of TDY. Officer,
  Airman dir to rtn as crew mbr to the place from which TDY originated.


  NAME                    RANK       AFSN          DUTY
  PETERSON, LOWELL, F.    CAPT       FV3126846     ACM UNQ
```

Orders for flight

four-engine passenger transport during takeoff and flight.

After my initial excitement, and a few hundred miles of flying at altitude, observing the operation on the flight deck, I decided to walk back through the passenger section. I guess I wasn't prepared for what I saw. The standard commercial passenger seating from front to back was filled with young, eighteen-to-twenty-year-old Marines, all dressed alike, in dark green uniforms with a tie pulled tight to the collar of a khaki shirt. Their almost identical youthful faces were topped off with a fresh, close-shaved marine haircut. Their demeanor was also identical. There were no smiles, no talking, and no horseplay so often expected from this age group. They were scared. They were going ten thousand miles from home, into combat, some of them making the last flight of their lives. I had no luck in striking up any conversations with any of them. They were courteous, and always answered with a, "Yes, Sir," or, "No, Sir." I wished them well, and returned to the flight deck in time for our approach into Da Nang.

We were on the ground in Da Nang long enough to refuel, unload our troops, let them claim their duffel bags, watch them line up in formation and be marched away, load up the aircraft with Marines being rotated back to the states, and load the cargo hold with their duffel bags. Unfortunately, also loaded into the cargo hold, were body bags of the casualities of war making their final journey. When we left Da Nang, I was again on the flight deck during takeoff. The pilot informed the crew that due to the possibility of unfriendly fire near the base, he was going to make a maximum performance takeoff. This was very exciting, as he set the airplane on its tail at a 25° angle as soon as we were off the ground. The Marines, who were used to being frightened, experienced a new lesson in fright.

However, as soon as we were airborne and the Marines realized they were really leaving Vietnam and going home, they let out a cheer that could compete with any college football stadium on a Saturday afternoon. In contrast to the mood on the flight to Da Nang, these Marines smiled, laughed, joked, horsed around, and fantasized about the first things they were going to do when they got home. I again left the flight deck and made my way through the aircraft from front to back, stopping to talk along the way. Some were willing to talk about their experiences on the battlefields of South Vietnam, but most just wanted to leave those memories behind.

As we approached Kadena AFB in our landing pattern, the airplane was again buzzing with conversation as they all leaned over one another, looking out the windows, to see a land where they knew they would not be under fire. As we touched down, another big cheer went up. I was sitting with a young Marine who was smiling from ear to ear. As he looked out the window, his first comment was, "green grass; mowed, green grass!" I realized that he had seen nothing but jungle for eighteen months. As we taxied up to the front of the terminal, his second comment was, "round-eyes!" I also realized that he had seen no non-Asian women in eighteen months. I felt good as I got off the airplane, knowing that at least this group of Marines was going home to mowed green grass and to their preference for women with round eyes, including those of their thankful mothers.

> Five times as many Marines died in Vietnam as in World War I, three times as many as in Korea, and the Marines suffered more total casualties, killed and wounded, in Vietnam than in all of World War II.
>
> The Marine Corps, which lost 103,000 killed or wounded out of some 400,000 sent to Vietnam, awarded 47 medals of honor (34 posthumously), 362 Navy Crosses (139 posthumously), and 2,592 Silver Stars.
>
> *The American Legion Magazine*
> September 2003

CITATION TO ACCOMPANY THE AWARD OF

THE AIR FORCE COMMENDATION MEDAL

TO

LOWELL F. PETERSON

Captain Lowell F. Peterson distinguished himself by meritorious service as Commander, Detachment 4, 1st Medical Service Wing, and as Flight Surgeon, 824th USAF Dispensary from 6 October 1963 to 28 February 1966. During this period, Captain Peterson demonstrated exceptional ability, resourcefulness, knowledge and efficiency while introducing progressive changes in management which permitted his unit to expeditiously deploy to numerous Southeast Asia locations. The distinctive accomplishments of Captain Peterson reflect credit upon himself and the United States Air Force.

BIOGRAPHIES

—

Jim Sandin

Jim Sandin was the youngest of seven children of Sigfred and Christine Sandin. He was born in Closter, Nebraska, and when he was six years old he moved with his parents to a farm near Newman Grove, Nebraska. He graduated from high school in 1955 as valedictorian, and then attended the University of Nebraska at Lincoln, where he graduated with distinction in 1960. Sandin entered pilot training at Vance Air Force Base in 1961 before going to Luke Air Force Base to transition into the F-100 as a fighter pilot. In 1963 he was assigned to Nellis Air Force Base to learn to fly the F-105. He was the first F-105 student without previous operational combat fighter squadron experience.

Jim Sandin

Following the grueling training program at Nellis, Sandin was assigned to Kadena Air Force Base, Okinawa, and during his Far East tour he was also deployed on temporary duty (TDY) to Southeast Asia where he flew combat missions over North Vietnam and Laos, receiving the Distinguished Flying Cross and the Air Medal with two Oak Leaf Clusters.

While TDY at Korat Air Force Base, Thailand, he developed an 80 percent hearing loss in his right ear, which disqualified him for flight status. Sandin, at that time also mentioned to the flight surgeon (Doc Peterson) that he had a persistent, recurrent pain that would shoot up his right leg, especially if he stubbed his foot on something. It was decided this should be checked out after the squadron returned to Kadena. Therefore, in late August 1965, in the course of trying to get back on flying status after his hearing difficulties, Sandin again mentioned his ongoing pain in his leg. After a thorough examination, no obvious abnormalities could be demonstrated and x-rays were ordered.

The x-rays revealed a large bony tumor on the front of the hip bone (femur) near the groin which appeared to be a possible osteosarcoma, a malignant bone tumor. Doc conferred with his medical colleagues and they agreed with the diagnosis.

Jim Sandin remembers the rest of the story this way: "It was late on Friday afternoon, and there was to be a 12th Squadron party at the Officers Club that evening. Doc found me there and told me he had discovered an abnormality on the x-ray, and asked me to meet him at the flight surgeon's office the next morning, which I did. We left there, x-rays in hand, and went to Camp Kue army hospital to be evaluated by a surgeon. The army surgeon agreed with the interpretation and recommended I be admitted to the hospital on Monday morning for excision of the tumor. This rapid course of events was a shock to me and my family.

"The surgeons removed the tumor from my leg, and in less than a week, I was med-evac'd to San Antonio's Wilford Hall USAF hospital. Before I left Okinawa, Colonel Cardenas, the 18th Wing Commander, and members of the 12th TFS came to the Camp Kue hospital, where I was presented with my combat decorations. The squadron gave me a portable Sony TV to watch during my recuperation. Capt. Frank Street was generous enough to sell our car and help my family pack for their return to the United States.

"I spent from early September until mid-November 1965 in rehabilitation, expecting to get back on flying status. But, before being released to duty, the orthopedic surgeon at Wilford Hall ordered more x-rays. The x-rays showed that a tumor as large, or larger, than the original had recurred. Another surgery was performed just before Thanksgiving. The tumor was adjacent to the femoral nerve, and to excise all of the tumor, the surgeon had to scrape the femoral nerve, and as a consequence, I was unable to extend my lower leg by its own power for over six months. I went home for Christmas hopeful my troubles were behind me, but, upon my return to the hospital in January 1966, I was informed that a third surgery was being considered. The physical therapist told me that they might have to amputate my leg. The tumor board had met during the Christmas week and the oncologist (cancer specialist) had convinced the board that the tumor was malignant and amputation was necessary if I was to have any chance of survival.

"A friend of mine in Denver, Jesse Miller, had awakened during the night before my return to the hospital and had felt a special need to pray about my condition. After an hour of prayer, he felt at peace and went back to sleep. In the morning, the doctors called the Armed Forces Institute of Pathology in Washington, DC, where the tumor had been sent for further analysis. The report from the Institute was that there was 'no conclusive evidence of malignancy'. I feel that it was an answer to prayer, that the colonel in charge of the orthopedic section took the word of the Institute rather than the recommendations of the oncologist at Wilford Hall. With extensive therapy, I was able to regain nerve and muscle function, and I have not had any significant negative effects of the tumor or of the operations during the many years since."

Sandin was released from medical follow-up in mid-1966 and was assigned to Medina Air Base as an instructor. He retired from the United States Air Force on November 21, 1968, and started working for Continental Airlines on December 9, 1968.

Sandin flew the B-727 and B-737 for Continental. Twenty of his thirty-two years there were spent as an instructor and conducting flight tests. He retired in December 2000.

Jim's wife Lori passed away in 1993. They had three children. Jim married Sharon Hulst in 1995, and they reside in Lincoln, California.

John Morrissey

John Morrissey was born in Kansas City, Missouri, on July 31, 1939. He graduated from the University of Kansas in the class of 1960, and was a civilian flight instructor and charter pilot from 1959 to 1961. Morrissey entered the United States Air Force (USAF) pilot training program at Larado AFB, Texas, in 1961, followed by USAF fighter training at Luke Field in Phoenix, Arizona, where he flew the F-100. He graduated first in his class in both programs. He received his checkout in the F-105 fighter-bomber at Nellis Air Force Base, Nevada, and was given his first operational assignment to the 12th Tactical Fighter Squadron, at Kadena Air Force Base, Okinawa, in September 1963. During this tour-of-duty, Morrissey flew combat missions in Vietnam and Laos while on TDY (temporary duty) to Southeast Asia.

John Morrissey

After leaving Kadena in April 1966, Morrissey completed a lengthy tour at the USAF Fighter Weapons School at Nellis AFB, Nevada, until 1969. He was then stationed at Luke Field as a test pilot in the A-7D test program while still assigned to the Fighter Weapons School. In 1971 Morrissey was transferred to Davis Monthan AFB, Tucson, Arizona, as flight commander, 354th TFS. In September 1972, he became flight commander of the 356th TFS, and took his flight TDY to Korat, Thailand. Morrissey later served as flight commander of the 3rd TFS at Korat until June 1973. Morrisey flew two hundred and forty-two combat missions between 1964 and 1973, with one hundred and forty over North Vietnam, and the majority of the rest over Laos. His last combat mission was in Cambodia on June 23, 1973.

After graduating from the Army Command and General Staff College in 1974, Morrissey served another three years on the faculty before assuming a five-year assignment as the USAF adviser to the South Dakota Air National Guard, stationed at Joe Foss Field, Sioux Falls, South Dakota. He was promoted to full colonel in January 1982. From 1982 until he retired on July 1, 1985, Morrissey was the USAF Tactical Air Command's senior representative to the U.S. Army Combined Arms Center. He is the recipient of the Legion of Merit, five Distinguished Flying Crosses, three Meritorious Service medals, the Air Medal with twelve Oak Leaf Clusters, and eight Vietnam Campaign medals. He is a member of the Red River Valley Fighter Pilot Association and previously was a member of the Society of Experimental Test Pilots.

In a recent interview, Morrissey stated, "I had the privilege in my career to work for Gen. Colin Powell, Gen. M. Anthony (Tony) McPeak, and Gen. Chuck Horner, who retired me on July 1, 1985. I could not have been blessed with a better career, been associated with finer people, or flown a finer airplane than the F-105. I feel very fortunate to have served in the United States Air Force."

While at the Army Staff College, Morrissey bought a biplane, which led him to enter the sport of aerobatics competition. He became the leader of the only four-ship civilian aerobatics team in the United States. In 1997, along with his son, Matt, he was on the last American aerobatic team to win a gold medal in international competition. Morrissey now owns and operates an aerobatics school in Grain Valley, Missouri, a suburb of Kansas City, using a special two-place instructor plane. He lives with his wife, Linda, in Lee's Summit, Missouri.

William J. Hosmer

William J. Hosmer was born October 17, 1930, in Rolette, North Dakota. He enlisted in the army in 1948 and one year later was admitted to the United States Military Academy at West Point, New York. He graduated with a Bachelor of Science degree in engineering on June 2, 1953, and was commissioned a second lieutenant in the United States Air Force.

Hosmer was assigned as an F-86 Sabre pilot with the 723rd Fighter-Bomber Squadron at Foster Field, Texas, before being reassigned in 1956 to the 311th F-86 Fighter-Bomber Squadron in Korea. In 1957 Hosmer became an F-100 Super Sabre instructor pilot with the 4520th Combat Crew Training Wing at Nellis Air Force Base, Nevada, and three years

William J. Hosmer

later was an F-100 instructor with the United States Air Force Fighter Weapons School. From 1961 to 1963, Hosmer flew the left wing position with the U.S. Air Force Thunderbirds aerial demonstration team.

From August 1963 to January 1966, Hosmer served with the 18th Tactical Fighter Wing at Kadena Air Force Base, Okinawa, as a F-105 Thunderchief pilot and commander of Lima Flight in the 12th TAC Fighter Squadron. During this tour, he flew tactical fighter-bomber missions over North Vietnam, South Vietnam, and Laos.

In January 1966, Hosmer entered the Armed Forces Staff College, and upon completion, earned the position of Chief, Fighter Branch, Tactical Air Command Directorate of Requirements at Langley Air Force Base, Virginia. In May 1969, Hosmer returned to Southeast Asia as the commander of the 308th Tactical Fighter Squadron at Tuy Hoa Airbase, South Vietnam, flying F-100s. In April 1970 he became the assistant director of operations, and later, deputy commander for operations of the 48th Tactical Fighter Wing at the Royal Air Force Base in

Lackenheath, England, again flying the F-100.

In May 1972, Hosmer returned to the United States and attended the Air War College at Maxwell Air Force Base in Alabama, where he graduated a year later. He then served as Vice Commander of the 355th Tactical Fighter Wing at Davis-Monthan Air Force Base, Arizona, until July 1974, when he assumed command of the Wing.

Colonel Hosmer retired in 1976, finishing his Air Force career as a command pilot with 240 combat missions. He was awarded the Silver Star, the Legion of Merit, and the Air Medal with 13 Oak Leaf Clusters. He is a member of the Daedalians, the Air Force Association, and the Red River Valley Fighter Pilots Association. He and his wife, Pat, are the parents of five grown children. Bill and Pat split their time between homes in Bottineau, North Dakota, and Tucson, Arizona.

Frank Tullo

Frank Tullo was born in Chicago in October 1939, the son of Italian immigrants. He graduated from St. Mel High School and finished two and one-half years of college at Wright Junior College, the University of Chicago, and the University of Illinois before joining the Air Force as an aviation cadet in October 1959. In college Tullo was an engineering major and worked part time at the Joseph T. Ryerson steel factory.

One evening, while visiting one of the original McDonald's restaurants on the north side of Chicago with his buddies, Tullo heard a loud noise in the sky. He looked up and saw four F-86 fighter jets of the Air National Guard flying out of O'Hare airport in a tight echelon formation. Tullo knew where he was going next. The following day he called an Air Force recruiter.

Tullo was assigned to fighter training at Luke Air Force Base in Arizona before being transferred to Nellis Air Force Base in Nevada. He served five years as a fighter pilot, flying F-100s and F-105s at Kadena Air Force Base in Okinawa. During this tour of duty, he flew combat missions over North Vietnam and Laos. Tullo was shot down and rescued on July 27, 1965, on the outskirts of Hanoi. He received the Distinguished Flying Cross, the Air Medal with Oak Leaf Cluster, and the Purple Heart.

Frank Tullo

After leaving Kadena, Tullo served for one year at McConnell Air Force Base, Wichita, Kansas, as an F-105 instructor pilot. He retired from the Air Force in September 1966 and became a pilot for Continental Airlines where he remained until retirement in 1999. During his career with Continental, Tullo finished a bachelor's degree, and went on to earn a master's degree in human factors from Pepperdine University in California.

NASA convinced the airline industry that human factors training was needed to concentrate on the "softer" side of flying skills—managing a team, situation awareness, communication, monitoring, assertiveness, etc. Thus, the discipline, taught at the graduate level, human factors, became a reality.

Tullo flew the Boeing 707, 727, 757/767, and the DC-10, DC-9, MD-80, Sabreliner, and Lear Jet. He was a flight engineer instructor, a flight instructor, a Boeing 727 fleet manager, a director of human factors, the chief pilot of Los Angeles and Honolulu, and the vice president of flight operations. He also represented Continental Airlines on many Air Transport Association (ATA) committees in Washington, DC, including the Flight Systems Integration Committee, Flight Operations Committee, and the Human Factors Committee.

Tullo is currently a part-time faculty member at Cal State University at Los Angeles, and Embry-Riddle Aeronautical University Extension. He has an aviation consultant business, specializing in human factors and in this capacity he works for domestic and foreign airlines, as well as for the United Space Alliance, the organization that maintains the space shuttle. Tullo is a member of the Civil Air Patrol and flies search-and-rescue missions in Southern California.

Frank Tullo and his wife, Linda, live in Palm Springs, California.

Paul Craw

Paul Craw was born in Stratton, Nebraska, on September 9, 1930. He graduated from Stratton High School and joined the Air Force cadets in 1952. He went to Nellis Air Force Base (AFB) in May of 1953 hoping to get into the Korean War, but the conflict ended while he was still in gunnery training. Craw did go to Korea after the war, and then was sent to Clovis AFB, New Mexico.

Paul Craw

Craw returned to Nellis AFB in February of 1963 for F-105 training and volunteered to fly a 105 to Kadena AFB, Okinawa, in late 1963. That was his first of nine Pacific crossings ferrying F-105s, each of which required multiple in-air refuelings.

Craw was involved in the first deployment with the 12th Tactical Fighter Squadron (TFS) from Kadena AFB to Da Nang, South Vietnam, in December 1964, and the evacuation to Korat, Thailand, in January 1965. He flew several combat missions prior to his squadron being replaced at Korat in February 1965, by the 67th TFS from Kadena AFB.

In March 1965 Craw was transferred to McConnell Air Force Base, Kansas, which he felt was the best thing that ever happened to him. Not long after arriving there, he was again sent on temporary duty assignment (TDY) to Southeast Asia with the McConnell 563rd TFS stationed at Takhli, Thailand. The TDY ended in August when his squadron was replaced by the 562 Squadron.

In late 1966 Craw went to Takhli as a permanent change of station and joined the 357th Squadron. On April, 14, 1967, the squadron was ordered to attack a steel mill in the Hanoi area. It was Craw's 121st combat mission in the F-105. Due to weather, the primary target was cancelled and he was directed to a secondary target in the Dien Bien Phu area. As Craw approached the target his plane was hit by antiaircraft fire. He delivered his bombs on target and bailed out. Upon landing, he sustained a compound fracture of his right leg. After successful rescue by the

"Jolly Green Giant" helicopter, Craw was transported to Laos and then to Udorn, Thailand, before being evacuated to Saigon, South Vietnam; Clark Air Force Base, in the Philippines; Andrews Air Force Base near Washington, DC; and finally to Scott Air Force Base, Illinois. He was hospitalized there for four months. One month after being discharged, Craw was back flying the F-105.

Craw returned to McConnell Air Force Base where he remained until 1971. He requested and received a check-out in the F-4 and went back to Da Nang, South Vietnam, for a year. Thereafter, Craw was at McDill Air Force Base for a short period of time before being assigned to Bitburg, Germany. Paul Craw retired from the U.S. Air Force in 1975 with the rank of Colonel.

After retirement from the Air Force, Craw worked as an instructor for Flight Safety at Citation Aircraft in Wichita, Kansas. His boss was Bob Wayne, who had been Craw's commander at Takhli in 1966. Craw retired in 1998 and is enjoying his retirement in Wichita.

Wes Schierman

Wesley D. Schierman was born in St. John, Washington, on July 21, 1935. During his senior year in high school, he joined the Washington State Air National Guard (ANG). One year later, in 1954, Schierman entered USAF pilot training, receiving his Wings and Commission at Williams Air Force Base, Arizona, on February 23, 1956. Following fighter gunnery training, he returned to the Washington ANG, flying F-94 and F-89 aircraft. From 1956 to 1958, Schierman attended Washington State University, graduating with a Bachelor of Science degree in psychology.

Wesley D. Schierman

In 1958 Wes Schierman married Faye Rigsby. Between 1958 and 1962, he was flying for Northwest Airlines and continuing his participation as a pilot for the ANG. In 1962 Captain Schierman returned to active duty, and was assigned to the 481st Tactical Fighter Squadron (TFS) at Cannon AFB, New Mexico, flying F-100 aircraft. In 1964 he was re-assigned to the 67th TFS at Kadena Air Force Base, Okinawa.

In 1965 Captain Schierman flew combat missions in Laos and North Vietnam. On August 28, 1965, his aircraft became disabled and he was forced to bail out near Son La. He was captured by the North Vietnamese and spent the next seven and one-half years as a POW.

Major Schierman was released from captivity on February 12, 1973. He resumed his career as a pilot for Northwest Airlines until his retirement in 1995. Wes and Faye reside in Everett, Washington, near their children and grandchildren. He continues to fly in his experimental RV-4.

12th TAC Fighter Squadron Personnel
January 1, 1965 - December 31, 1965

Lieutenant Colonel Charles W. Reed, Commander

Lieutenant Colonel Robert L. Fair, Operations Officer

Major Paul S. Cleland, Jr., Assistant Operations Officer

Captain Robert B. Purcell, Weapons Officer

India Flight

Captain Charles R. Copin, Flight Commander

Captain Vernon E. "Gene" Frank

Captain Thomas E. Boatman

Captain George A. Bogert

Captain Matthew J. Kelch, Jr.

Captain Samuel E. Waters, Jr.

First Lieutenant John C. Morrissey

Juliette Flight

Captain Dana B. Cromack, Flight Commander

Captain Allen L. Anderson

Captain Robert N. Daughtery

Captain Charles M. Yeokum

Captain Wesley G. Carey, Jr.

Captain Robert M. Crane

First Lieutenant Charles C. Large

Kilo Flight

Major Ralph H. Bowersox, Flight Commander

Captain Donald F. Smith

Captain Raymond V. Moss

Captain John H. Busbee

First Lieutenant James R. Hostetter

First Lieutenant James K. Sandin

Lima Flight

Major William J. Hosmer, Flight Commander

Captain Don I. Williamson

Captain John C. Jones

First Lieutenant Frank J. Tullo

First Lieutenant Charles G. Hofelich

UNASSIGNED

Captain Pike G. Grubbs

Captain Anatole Semenov, Jr.

Captain John F. Rehm

Compiled by W. H. Plunkett, Albuquerque, NM

BIBLIOGRAPHY

Herrig, George C. *America's Longest War, The United States and Vietnam 1950-1975*, Second Edition. New York, NY: Alfred A. Knopf.

Halberstam, David. *The Best and Brightest, Twentieth-Anniversary Edition*. New York, NY: Ballantine Books.

Vietnam—25th Anniversary Commemorative. Five Star Publications.

Bell, Brig. Gen. Ken, USAF (Ret.). *100 Missions North—A Fighter Pilot's Story of the Vietnam War*. Paducah, KY: Turner Publishing Co.

McNamara, Robert S. with Brian Van De Mark. *In Retrospect—The Tragedy and Lessons of Vietnam*. New York, NY: Vintage Books, a division of Random House, 1995.

Guarino, Col. Larry. *A P.O.W.'s Story: 2801 Days in Hanoi*. New York, NY: Ivy Books, 1990.

DeMille, Nelson. *Up Country*. New York, NY: Warner Vision Books, 2002.

Kinzey, Bert. *F-105 Thunderchief*. Blue Ridge Summit, PA: Aero, a division of TAB BOOKS Inc.

Blagov, Sergei. *VIETNAM* magazine. August 2001, p.26-32. "Missile Ambushes: Soviet Air Defense Aid."

VIETNAM magazine February 2001, p.21.

National Geographic Vol. 128, No.3, September 1965. National Geographic Society, Washington, DC.

INFLIGHT Air Wisconsin. April-May 1984. Meridian Publishing Co.

FALCON, Vol. 4, No. 18. Kadena, Okinawa, May 6, 1965.

Laird, Melvin R. *Iraq: Learning the Lessons of Vietnam*. Foreign Affairs: Vol. 84, No.6, Nov/Dec 2005 p.22-43.

Lance Morrow. *Time* magazine Vol. 125, No. 15, Apr.15, 1985.

Time magazine. All issues 1964-1966.

Prize: Berry, B. Frank. *U.S. Medicine Information Central*. U.S. Medicine Inc. 2000-2005.

Murphy, Edward F. *VIETNAM MEDAL of HONOR HEROES*. New York, NY: Ballantine Books, 1987.

World Book, The. Encyclopedia, 1988 Edition. World Book, Inc.

Red River Valley Fighter Pilot Association. *NAM POW Symposium*. Las Vegas, NV, 2003.

PBS DVD Video. *Return with Honor, THE AMERICAN EXPERIENCE*. Boston, MA: WGBH, 2001.

Stevens, Michael E., *Voices from Vietnam*. Chapt. 6 "Prisoners of War", pgs. 157-181. State Historical Society of Wisconsin, 1996.

Auchincloss, Louis. *Theodore Roosevelt*, Time Books 2001. Henry Holt and Company LLC.

www.wikipedia.com

www.google.com

Medal of Honor - Portraits of Valor Beyond the Call of Duty, ©2003, The Congressional Medal of Honor Foundation.

EPILOGUE

Hilton opens five-star hotel in Hanoi thirty plus years later

No longer silver, the F-105s fly into retirement in combat camouflage

Operation Air Boon Choo, April 1964

SEATO EXERCISE AIR BOON CHOO

For participating in SEATO Tactical Air Exercise
AIR BOON CHOO
held in Thailand from **20** through **30** April **1964**
the Exercise Director expresses his appreciation to

LOWELL F. PETERSON, CAPT. USAF (MC)

whose dedicated conduct and display of professional skills
contributed to the success of the Exercise and strengthened
the bonds of friendship between member nation Air Forces.

Panneng Kantarat
Panneng Kantarat
Air Vice Marshal
Royal Thai Air Force
Exercise Director

Bangkok   April 1964

Operation Air Boon Choo

Operation Air Boon Choo, April 1964 (continued)

Sunset over Camp Nasty

Lineup for the mess hall at Camp Nasty (left) and washing utensils (right, foreground)

Thai women doing our laundry

Camp Nasty

Camp Nasty hooches and boardwalk

Det. 4 Dispensary

We Go to War - 1965

THIRTY-FIVE CENTS

APRIL 23, 1965

WHO'S FIGHTING IN VIET NAM
A Gallery of American Combatants

TIME

THE WEEKLY NEWSMAGAZINE

AIR FORCE
PILOT RISNER

VOL. 85 NO. 17

See story on page 36

(Left to right): Bill Joyce, Jay Mitchell, Don Williamson, Frank Tullo, Bob Purcell, and Bill Hosmer
Note the Presidential Unit Citation awarded to the 18th TFW emblazoned on the fuselage of the F-105
(below the letters U.S.).

Don Williamson

Frank Tullo

Korat AFB - July 1965

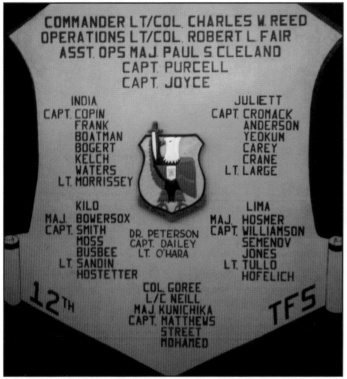

COMMANDER LT/COL. CHARLES W. REED
OPERATIONS LT/COL. ROBERT L. FAIR
ASST. OPS MAJ. PAUL S. CLELAND
CAPT. PURCELL
CAPT. JOYCE

INDIA
CAPT. COPIN
FRANK
BOATMAN
BOGERT
KELCH
WATERS
LT. MORRISSEY

JULIETT
CAPT. CROMACK
ANDERSON
YEOKUM
CAREY
CRANE
LT. LARGE

KILO
MAJ. BOWERSOX
CAPT. SMITH
MOSS
BUSBEE
LT. SANDIN
HOSTETTER

DR. PETERSON
CAPT. DAILEY
LT. O'HARA

LIMA
MAJ. HOSMER
CAPT. WILLIAMSON
SEMENOV
JONES
LT. TULLO
HOFELICH

COL. GOREE
L/C NEILL
MAJ. KUNICHIKA
CAPT. MATTHEWS
STREET
MOHAMED

12TH   TFS

12th TAC Sign courtesy of Andy Anderson

*Doc Peterson and Col. Chuck Reed,
Commander 12th TFS, Korat,
July 1965*

*Back: Unkown, Fair, Bowersox, Anderson, Daughtery, Busby, Morrissey, unknown, O'Hara, Moss, Purcell, Hosmer
Front: Frank, Reed, Boo Boo, Hofelich, Large, Yeokum*

Korat AFB - July 1965 (continued)

New "O" Club bar

*The old "O" Club at Korat. Paul Cleland,
Charlie Copin, Sam Waters, Bill Hosmer*

The new Officers Club

Paul Cleland and Capt. Bailey discuss the war. Capt. Kunichika in background

Charlie Copin, Harry Matthews, Sam Waters, and Matt Kelch

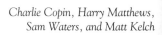

Korat Air Force Base, 1965

Korat AFB - July 1965 (continued)

F-105s

Gene Frank, Korat,
(cigar always present)

F-105s flight of four returning from a mission

Bill Joyce, Tony Semenov, Bill Hosmer, Chuck Hofelich ready for a sortie

Ray Moss and Gene Frank

Doc at the flight line

Lt. Col. Robert Fair
Operations Officer

Col. Chuck Reed

Jim Hostetter, Bill Hosmer, Ralph Bowersox,
and Jim Sandin (kneeling)

Paul Kunichika, John Busby,
and Chuck Large

*Doc and wife Mary, at airport in Saigon on the way to Bangkok,
hard to believe there is a war on*

*Stewardess in Ao-dai dress,
Saigon*

*Doc on R&R July 24, 1965,
with daughter, Linda
(Day of first SAM attack)*

*The future Dr. Linda Peterson and "Doc" Peterson
at Kadena Circle House, Jan. 1965*

Singapore

View from the U.S. Air Attaché's house, Singapore, Sept. 1965

British Dispensary, Singapore

Singapore

(continued)

The Doctor in charge, Tengah, Singapore-RAF

British Pilots in Singapore

Major Hosmer (red shirt) speaks with British pilots

Reception at Air Attaché Villa (Col. Cardenas, 18th TFW Commander, second from right)

Bill Hosmer and Charlie Copin

Reunion of the River Rats 2005-2006

Ralph "Sox" and Barbara Bowersox

Harry Matthews

Bill Hosmer and Doc Peterson

Jimmie Ginger and Tom Lockhart with their wives (44th Squadron)

"Moose" Skowron 44th Squadron

Joan and Chuck Hofelich and Jane Copin

Peggy and Frank Street

Charlie Copin with Jane and John Morrisey

Reunion of the River Rats
2005-2006 *(continued)*

Turk Turley

*Col. "Dag" Damewood
and wife, Jean*

Jim Sandin and Doc Peterson

Matt Kelch and Frank Tullo

*Dr. Jerry Unatin, Will Snell (44th Squadron),
and Dr. Lowell Peterson*

Doc, Harry, Bill, and Chuck

George Peacock

J. C. Jones

Jane and Charlie Copin and Pat Hosmer

Mr. and Mrs. Andy Anderson

Bud Day

In Vietnam, George E. "Bud" Day, WWII and Korean War veteran, became a top-secret Misty-Super FAC, a forward air controller with the task of identifying military targets and arranging air strikes to destroy them. He was shot down and captured on August 27, 1967, but managed to escape and evaded capture for 15 days. His resistance to the enemy and his POW resistance efforts after re-capture earned him the Medal of Honor. He was repatriated on March 14, 1973.

Medal of Honor Recipient, former POW, Col. "Bud" Day

Back: Charlie Copin, Matt Kelch, Paul Craw, J. C. Jones, and Doc Peterson
Front: Bill Hosmer, Chuck Hofelich, Jim Hostetter, and Frank Tullo

40th Reunion, July 27, 2005. Remembering the Rescue of Dogwood Two

Bill Hosmer, Doc Peterson, Frank Tullo, Holt Livesay, Ed Greatbach, George Martin

Holt Livesay and Ed Greatbach beside the A-1E Skyraider

Mr. and Mrs. Holt Livesay

Mr. and Mrs. George Martin

Mr. and Mrs. Frank Tullo

George Martin and Frank Tullo by the "Jolly Green Giant" Helicopter

Mr. and Mrs. Ed Greatbach